GUIDELINES

THE THREE WEEKS

GUIDELINES

Over Four Hundred
of the Most Commonly
Asked Questions about
THE THREE WEEKS

Rabbi Elozor Barclay
Rabbi Yitzchok Jaeger

TARGUM/FELDHEIM

First published 2003
Second edition published 2004
Copyright © 2003, 2004 by E. Barclay & Y. Jaeger
ISBN 1-56871-254-5

Please address any questions or comments
regarding these notes to the authors:
E. Barclay (02) 583 0914
Y. Jaeger (02) 583 4889
email: yjaeger@barak-online.net

By the same authors:
GUIDELINES TO PESACH
GUIDELINES TO THE YOMIM NORAIM
GUIDELINES TO SUCCOS
GUIDELINES TO CHANUKAH
GUIDELINES TO PURIM
GUIDELINES TO FAMILY PURITY

Published by:
Targum Press, Inc.
22700 W. Eleven Mile Rd.
Southfield, MI 48034
E-mail: targum@netvision.net.il
Fax toll free: (888) 298-9992

Distributed by:
Feldheim Publishers
200 Airport Executive Park
Nanuet, NY 10954
www.feldheim.com

Printed in Israel

Rabbi CHAIM P. SCHEINBERG

Rosh Hayeshiva "TORAH ORE"

and Morah Hora'ah of Kiryat Mattersdorf

הרב חיים פינחס שיינברג

ראש ישיבת ״תורה אור״

ומורה הוראה דקרית מטרסדורף

בס״ד, חודש שבט, תשס״ג

מכתב ברכה

I was pleased to see "**Guidelines**", an impressive six volume work which encompasses the *halachos* of the *Moadim* and other relevant topics, written by Rabbi Elozor Barclay, *shlita* and Rabbi Yitzchok Jaeger, *shlita*. These books have been praised highly by numerous *Gedolei HaRabbonim* and have been received warmly by the English speaking Torah community.

As a matter of policy, I do not endorse *halachic* rulings in any published *sefer*. However, since so many *Gedolei Torah* have already agreed to what is written and offered their approbation to "**Guidelines**", I join them and offer my heartfelt blessing that *Hashem* should guide and assist the authors in producing more successful *halachic* works, which glorify and strengthen the Torah.

Signed in the honor of the Torah,

Rabbi Chaim Pinchas Scheinberg

רחוב פנים מאירות 2, ירושלים, ת.ד. 6979, טל. 537-1513 (02), ישראל

2 Panim Meirot St., Jerusalem, P.O.B. 6979, Tel. (02) 537-1513, Israel

משה הלברשטאם

חבר הבד"צ העדה החרדית

ראש ישיבת "דברי חיים" טשאקאווע

מח"ס שו"ת "דברי משה"

פעיה"ק ירושלים תובב"א

רח' יואל 8 טל. 5370514

בס"ד

ערב ט"ו בשבט לסדר "והיה ביום הששי" תשס"ג לפ"ק

מאד שמחתי ונהנתי כשהובאו לפני ליקוטים נפלאים לעת עתה על הלכות פורים, פסח, ימים נוראים, סוכה וחנוכה ואי"ה עוד יד נטוי' להשלים המלאכה, שחיברו האברכים החשובים חו"ב מוהר"ר אלעזר ברקלי שליט"א ומוהר"ר יצחק ייגר שליט"א אוצר בלום מה שאספו וליקטו הלכות רבות ונחוצות מהשו"ע ונושאי כליו מספרי הפוסקים ראשונים ואחרונים מסודר בתבונה והשכל בטטו"ד לתועלת וזיכוי הרבים.

ונוכחתי לראות כי הלכו מישרים לאסוקי שמעתתא אליבא דהלכתא והיטב אשר עשו שציינו מקור לכל הלכה והלכה למען אשר כבר הזהירו גאוני קדמאי שלא לפסוק הלכה למעשה מספרי הקיצורים.

ואמינא לפעלא טבא יישר כוחם וחילם לאורייתא והנני נותן להם בזה ברכת מו"ר הגה"צ שליט"א שיזכו להמשיך לעלות במעלות התורה להו"ל עוד חיבורים יקרים ולזכות את הרבים מתוך נחת ושפע ברכות והצלחה, אכי"ר.

ובעה"ח בפקודת הקודש

יהונתן וינר

מו"ץ בבית הוראה

שע"י מרן הגה"צ שליט"א

נ.ב. בספר על הלכות חנוכה שאלה 15, בגדר איסור מלאכה לנשים בחנוכה עיין בן איש חי פרשת וישב סי' כז, וט"ז ס' תרע סק"ב דמשמע דומיא דר"ח, וכן שמעתי מכרכא דכולי ביה מרא דכולא תלמודא (לשון מוהר"ר הגה"צ בשו"ת דברי משה ס' יד) ממוהר"ר חיים קנייבסקי שליט"א.

Letter of Approbation received from
Rabbi Nachman Bulman zt"l for Guidelines to Succos

Rabbi Nachman Bulman
Yeshivat Ohr Somayach
Beit Knesset Nachliel

רב נחמן בולמן
מנהל רוחני ישיבת אור שמח
רב ק"ק נחליאל נוה יעקב מזרח

בע"ה

יום ו', י"ח תמוז, תשס"ב פה עיה"ק ת"ו

Friday, eighteenth of Tammuz, 5672, the holy city of
Yerushalayim.

I was delighted to see the fifth volume of the
Guidelines series. The questions and answers in
Guidelines provide a clear and easily understood
format and clarify relevant halachic issues.

It is clear from the quality of this work that Rabbi
Elozor Barclay and Rabbi Yitzchok Jaeger have
invested great amounts of time and effort in their
thorough investigation of these dinim. Every
answer has been written carefully and thoughtfully,
considering both the classic and the most up-to-
date halachic authorities. The accurate Hebrew
references will certainly be an invaluable aid for
any reader who wishes to investigate further.

I highly recommend this book to any person who is
truly searching to know the correct conduct.

Signed with admiration,

נחמן בולמן

מנהל רוחני ישיבת אור שמח
רב ק"ק נחליאל נוה יעקב מזרח ביום הנ"ל
ועיני נשואות לשמים להסכמת שוכן במרומים

בית המדרש
לאסוקי שמעתתא

בס"ד

מכתב ברכה

הנני בא לברך הני תרי צנתרי דדהבא הרב אלעזר ברקלי
שליט"א והרב יצחק ייגר שליט"א, ת"ח העמלים לאסוקי
שמעתתא אליבא דהילכתא שנים ע"ג שנים ואשר יראתם
קודמת לחכמתם, ובאים לזכות את הרבים בהלכה צרופה
ומבוררת ליסודותיה ופרטיה, ולהדריך את ישראל המעשה
אשר יעשון אשר רבים כבר נהנו מתורתם.

וזכיתי להצטרף למצות זיכוי הרבים והרבצת התורה הנ"ל
כאשר עברתי על כל שאלה ותשובה בבירור ובדיוק פרטי
ההלכה ולהעיר ולהאיר במקום הנראה, וכל הרואה יווכח
בס"ד המיוחדת אשר המה זכו לפרוס את סבכי ההלכה
כשמלה לאחר שזכו לאמר על חכמה אחותי את.

והנני בתפילה ובברכה שיזכו שרבים יהנו מתורתם
ושיתגלגל על ידיהם ריבוי קיום התורה בעולם, ולזכות
בברכת מזכי הרבים ויזהירו כזוהר הרקיע ומצדיקי הרבים
ככוכבים לעולם ועד.

החותם בברכת התורה לומדיה ומקיימיה

יצחק קויפמן

ראש כולל לאסוקי שמעתתא, מו"ץ ברמות

בית המדרש לאסוקי שמעתתא - Beis Medrash La'asukai Sh'maisa
רמות פולין 52/10 - ירושלים - Ramot Polin 52/10 - Jerusalem
טל. Tel. 972-2-571 0971 / 586 2547

הרב רפאל צבי ובר
רב דקהילת קמניץ
ונוה יעקב מזרח, ירושלים

ז' כסלו תשס"ד
בס"ד

מכתב ברכה

שמחתי לראות ששני תלמידי חכמים יקרים הרב אלעזר ברקלי שליט"א והרב יצחק ייגר שליט"א חיברו ספר פסקי הלכות בשפה האנגלית.

וכבר זכו לחבר פסקי הלכות על המועדים שהתפרסמו הרבה, וזיכו את הרבים. ויש תועלת רבה בצורת הכתיבה בלשון שאלות ותשובות ועי"ז מתבררת ההלכה היטב.

ואע"פ שאיני מבין שפה האנגלית, אבל אני מכירם ויודעם בהשתדלות לאסוקי שמעתתא אליבא דהלכתא, ונשאו ונתנו אתי בהרבה נושאים, והנני מברכם שיקבלו דבריהם בביהמ"ד.

בברכת התורה,

צבי ובר

RABBI ZEV LEFF
Rabbi of Moshav Matisyahu
Rosh Hayeshiva Yeshiva Gedola Matisyahu

בס"ד
כ"ב סיון תשס"ב

It is with great pleasure that I have received the latest addition to the series of Halachic Guides produced by Rabbi Elozor Barclay שליט"א and Rabbi Yitzchok Jaeger שליט"א - **Guidelines** to Succos.

This is an impressive work which will serve as an invaluable aid to those who seek to be guided through this important period of the Jewish year.

As in the previous volumes the laws are lucidly and concisely presented in a manner that will serve as a guide and source for the beginner and a source of review for the advanced student. I highly recommend this work as all the other volumes of this series.

May Hashem grant the authors long life and health and ability to continue to merit Klal Yisroel with the promulgation of Torah and mitzvos.

With Torah blessings,

Rabbi Zev Leff

Table of Contents

Foreword

With mixed feelings of joy and sadness, we present a basic guide to the laws of The Three Weeks. On the one hand we give praise and express gratitude to Hashem for enabling us to compile this work, and to the public for receiving so warmly all our books on the laws of the Yomim Tovim. But on the other hand, we feel pain and sorrow that the Jewish nation is still in exile, and that the laws of the three weeks are still necessary.

One of the thirteen principles of our faith is to believe in the coming of the *moshiach*, and to wait eagerly for his arrival. Until that time, it is incumbent upon us to mourn over the destruction of the holy Temples and the terrible persecutions suffered by the Jewish people throughout the ages. By experiencing three weeks of mourning, our desire and yearning for the redemption will be aroused, and we will thereby become worthy to witness the rebuilding of the holy Temple.

Rarely will a written work be a perfect substitute for a one-to-one discussion with a rav. The answer to a query often depends upon various factors that only further questioning can clarify. Even though much thought and effort has been invested in the phrasing and wording used, it is possible that *halachos* may be misunderstood or misconstrued. Accordingly, any doubts that arise should be discussed with one's local rav. Our primary intent is to guide the reader through the maze of laws and customs that abound during these three weeks, hence the title GUIDELINES.

We would like to thank a few individuals, whose contribution to this book was of major significance. First and foremost, the great *posek* and community leader, *HaGaon* Rav Nachman Bulman, zt"l. Rav Bulman was a source of great encouragement when the series of GUIDELINES was launched, and this book is imbued with his invaluable perspective, reliability, and practicality.

Two exceptional *talmidei chachomim* graciously took time from their busy schedules to help turn this book into a reality. Rav Yirmiyahu Kaganoff, *shlita*, *posek* in *Neveh Yaakov*, thoroughly checked the entire manuscript, providing many invaluable comments and insights. His observations have left their impression on much of the book. We would also like to express our thanks to Rav Yitzchok Kaufman *shlita*, *Rosh Kollel La'asukei Sh'maisa* and *posek* in *Ramot*. His keen perception and comprehensive mastery of the topic provided many valuable changes and additions throughout the entire book.

Thanks are also due to Rabbi Moshe Dombey and all the staff at Targum Press, who have once again demonstrated their professional expertise with the production of this book.

It is our hope that in the merit of keeping the laws of the three weeks punctiliously, we will be worthy to see the fulfillment of the words of our Sages: "Whoever mourns over Jerusalem will be rewarded to witness its rejoicing".

Elozor Barclay   Yitzchok Jaeger
Yerushalayim, Iyar 5763

Chapter One

Introduction

1. What are 'The Three Weeks'?

The period between the seventeenth of Tammuz and the ninth of Av (Tisha b'Av) is known as 'The Three Weeks'. Throughout the generations, the Jewish nation has suffered numerous tragedies and calamities during these days, and the period has therefore become a time of mourning and introspection. In particular, we mourn the loss of the two holy Temples, both of which were destroyed on the ninth of Av (in the years 3338 and 3828). The opening and closing days of the three weeks are public fasts.

2. How is one required to mourn?

The mourning is observed by the restriction of joyous activities. These restrictions increase in severity as the period progresses, reaching a climax of intense mourning on Tisha b'Av. One can discern four different periods of time during the three weeks:

- From the seventeenth of Tammuz until *Rosh Chodesh* Av.
- From *Rosh Chodesh* Av until the week in which Tisha b'Av occurs.
- From the Sunday before Tisha b'Av (referred to throughout the book as "the week of Tisha b'Av").
- Tisha b'Av.

Certain restrictions also apply on the day following Tisha b'Av.

Important note: There are many differences between Ashkenazic and Sephardic customs during this period, and this presentation is for Ashkenazim only.

3. Are there any restrictions on the eve of the seventeenth of Tammuz?

According to most opinions, all the restrictions of the three weeks begin at nightfall on the eve of the seventeenth of Tammuz.

Chapter Two

The Seventeenth of Tammuz

4. Why is this day a public fast?

Five major tragedies occurred on this day:

- The first set of stone tablets were broken when *Moshe Rabbeinu* descended from Mount Sinai and saw the Jewish people worshipping the golden calf.
- The daily sacrifices ceased during the first holy Temple, since sheep were no longer available due to the siege.
- The walls of Jerusalem were breached prior to the destruction of the second holy Temple.
- A *sefer Torah* was burned by a wicked gentile named Apostumus, during the days of the second holy Temple.
- An idol was placed in the holy Temple.

5. What is the purpose of fasting?

The purpose of a public fast is to arouse one's heart to repentance, and to recall one's misdeeds and the similar misdeeds of our forefathers that caused such calamities. Each person is obligated to examine his ways on this day and undertake to repent from his errors. The fasting is not the actual goal, but only a means to the true goal of repentance. Regarding the sinful people of Nineveh, the verse says "And Hashem saw their actions"; our Sages comment that it does not say that Hashem saw their fasting but rather their actions. People who fast but waste the day with strolls and idle chatter have missed the main point. Nevertheless, it is not sufficient to repent without fasting, since the four public fasts have been decreed by the Prophets. (The four days are the seventeenth of Tammuz, Tisha b'Av, the fast of *Gedaliah* on the third of Tishrei, and the tenth of Teves.)

6. Is there any special mitzvah to perform on the fast?

There is a custom to give charity before *mincha*. This is advised by the verse that is read in the *haftarah*, "Keep justice and do charity" (*Yeshayahu* 51:1). Some have the custom to give at least the amount of money that would have been spent for meals on that day.

7. Do women need to fast?

Girls over bas mitzvah and women are obligated to fast if they are well. However, certain communities are lenient for this fast, particularly if she is weak or finds fasting difficult. A rav should be consulted.

8. Do pregnant or nursing women have to fast?

Strictly speaking they do not need to fast, since they do not usually have their full strength and fasting will be difficult for them. A woman who feels that she is strong enough is permitted to fast. If she feels weak during the fast she should certainly break the fast and eat. A woman who has given birth or miscarried (ח"ו) within thirty days should not fast even if she feels strong enough to do so.

9. What if a person is not feeling well?

A person who is ill is not permitted to fast, even if his illness is not serious. When the fast is postponed from Shabbos to Sunday one may be more lenient, and even a person who is only slightly ill does not need to fast. If he is not sure about his physical condition, he should consult a doctor.

10.   Are a *chosson* and *kallah* required to fast?

A *chosson* and *kallah* must fast, even if the fast occurs during the first week of their marriage.

11.   Should children be trained to fast?

No, children below bar/bas mitzvah do not need to fast even for a few hours. Nevertheless, if they understand that it is a day of mourning, they should be given only simple foods and certainly not treats.

12.   If a person is not required to fast, should he delay eating for a few hours?

No, this is not necessary and he may eat immediately in the morning.

13. May such a person eat as much as he likes?

No. In order to participate in the public fast day, he should limit himself to a sufficient amount of simple foods.

14. Should anything be done in place of fasting by someone who is exempt?

It is correct to give money to charity instead. Pregnant and nursing women do not need to do this.

15. How should a person who is fasting take medicine if required?

A person may swallow bitter or tasteless medicines in tablet, capsule, or liquid form, but not if they are pleasant tasting. The medicine should be taken without water or with a bitter tasting liquid. (If the medicine will still be effective when mixed with water, this is a practical solution since such liquid is usually bitter tasting.) If these alternatives are not feasible, he may take the medicine with a small amount of water, if refraining from doing so will cause illness or great discomfort.

16. Is a person who is fasting permitted to taste food and spit it out?

This is usually forbidden. However, it is permitted to taste a small quantity of food that is being prepared for a *seudas* mitzvah after the fast. One should spit out the food and be careful not to swallow any. A *b'racha* should not be recited.

17.   May the mouth be rinsed?

One may rinse the mouth with water or mouthwash only if a bad taste causes discomfort. Only a small amount of liquid should be used while leaning forward in order to ensure that it is not swallowed.

18.   May the teeth be cleaned?

The teeth may be cleaned with a dry toothbrush. Toothpaste may be used only if the bad taste in the mouth causes discomfort (see previous question).

19.   May one eat early in the morning before the fast begins?

The fast begins at *halachic* dawn and one may eat until this time. However, before going to sleep the previous evening, one must have in mind that he wishes to eat before dawn. A person who wakes up unexpectedly and did not intend to eat before dawn may not do so. However, if a person forgot to have it in mind or woke up unexpectedly, he may **drink** before dawn, even though it is still preferable to have it in mind from the previous evening.

20.   How close to *halachic* dawn may one begin to eat?

If one wishes to eat more than a *kebeitza* of bread or cake, he must begin at least thirty minutes before *halachic* dawn. One may begin to eat other foods or drinks even within this period. Women are not restricted by this thirty-minute limit even for bread or cake.

21.   What if a person recited a *b'racha* on food or drink and then realized that it is a fast day?

He should say ברוך שם כבוד מלכותו לעולם ועד and not eat or drink anything.

22.   If a person accidentally ate or drank what should he do?

He must stop immediately and continue to fast for the rest of the day. He is not obligated to fast on another day, but if he wishes to gain atonement for his mistake he may do so. If this is difficult, he may give a reasonable sum of money to charity.

23.   May such a person still say *aneinu* in *shemoneh esrei*?

Yes, but if he ate a *kezayis* of food or drank a cheekful of drink he should alter the wording slightly and say ביום צום התענית הזה.

24.   May a person who is exempt from fasting (e.g. ill, pregnant, a child etc.) say *aneinu* in *shemoneh esrei*?

No, he should omit the paragraph completely.

25.   What if a person forgot to say *aneinu*?

If he has already concluded the *b'racha* of *shema koleinu*, he should continue and say *aneinu* just before the verse *yihyu leratzon* at the end of *shemoneh esrei*. If he forgot there also, *shemoneh esrei* is not repeated.

26.   Are there any changes to *shemoneh esrei*?

At *mincha*, the following changes are made:

- A person who is fasting should say the paragraph *aneinu* in the *b'racha* of *shema koleinu*.
- *Sim shalom* is said instead of *shalom rav*, even if one is not fasting, nor *davening* with a *minyan*.
- A person who is fasting should say a special prayer before the end of *shemoneh esrei*. This begins רבון כל העולמים גלוי וידוע לפניך.

27.   May *avinu malkeinu* be said without a *minyan* or if one is not fasting?

Yes.

28.   Must *selichos* be recited with a *minyan*?

Although it is preferable to do so, it is not essential. An individual may recite *selichos* but should omit the thirteen attributes of mercy. Alternatively, the thirteen attributes may be chanted with the tune of the Torah reading, in which case one should continue until the end of the verse (*Shemos* 34:7).

29.   Is bathing permitted?

The custom is to refrain from bathing one's body with hot water. It is permitted to wash one's face, hands, and feet with hot water, and to shower one's body with cold water.

Chapter Three

The Three Weeks

30. What is forbidden during the three weeks?

The following three activities are forbidden:

- Weddings.
- Playing or listening to music.
- Haircuts.

31. Are engagements permitted?

One may become engaged during the entire three weeks. A festive meal may be held until *Rosh Chodesh*, but only light refreshments may be served between *Rosh Chodesh* and Tisha b'Av. In either case, music may not be played.

32. Which type of music is forbidden?

One may not play or listen to any musical instrument during the three weeks. It is also forbidden to listen to music on the radio or on a cassette. According to most opinions, this applies even to a *seudas* mitzvah such as a *bris, pidyon haben, sheva brachos, siyum,* or bar mitzvah.

33.   May one learn or teach to play an instrument?

This is usually forbidden. However, if the cancellation of lessons will cause a financial loss to the teacher, some opinions are lenient until the week of Tisha b'Av. A student may only practice to play the instrument if extra lessons would be required due to the break and he is not playing for the enjoyment. In any event, he must not practice during the week of Tisha b'Av.

34.   May one listen to a cassette of singing without music?

According to most opinions, this is also forbidden.

35.   May one sing without musical accompaniment?

It is permitted to sing:
- On Shabbos.
- At a *seudas* mitzvah.
- Songs of praise or arousal to serve Hashem.
- To young children.

Singing for pleasure is permitted until *Rosh Chodesh*, but it is preferable to refrain.

36.   May one dance without musical accompaniment?

Dancing is usually forbidden. However, at a *seudas* mitzvah some opinions allow dancing without music.

37.   May women have a haircut?

Generally speaking, both men and women are forbidden to have a haircut during the three weeks. However, a married woman may remove excess hair that protrudes out of her hair covering if necessary.

38.   May children have a haircut?

Ideally, children should also not have a haircut. If necessary, a child may have a haircut until the week of Tisha b'Av.

39.   May a boy have his first haircut (*chalakah*) when reaching the age of three?

Although some opinions permit it, the custom is to give the first haircut before or after the three weeks.

40.   May a man shave?

A man is forbidden to shave or trim his beard during the three weeks. A man who shaves daily and is liable to incur a financial loss if he refrains may shave until the week of Tisha b'Av. Nevertheless, he may not shave simply to avoid embarrassment. A rav should be consulted about shaving during the week of Tisha b'Av.

41.   May a man trim his mustache?

This is permitted only if it interferes with his eating. According to some opinions, even this is forbidden in the week of Tisha b'Av.

42.   May a woman shave her legs?

This is usually forbidden. However, according to some opinions, a married woman or a girl of marriageable age may be lenient, if she considers it to be necessary.

43.   May a woman pluck her eyebrows?

Yes.

44.   May one shave or have a haircut in honor of a *bris*?

According to most opinions, the parents of the child, the *sandek*, and the *mohel* may shave and have a haircut in honor of the *bris*. This is only permitted until the week of Tisha b'Av and only on the day of the *bris*. If the *bris* is held on Shabbos, they may shave and have a haircut on Friday.

45.   May one shave or have a haircut in honor of a *pidyon haben*?

No.

46.   May a boy have a haircut in honor of his bar mitzvah?

Ideally, he should not have a haircut. If necessary, he may have a haircut before his birthday until the week of Tisha b'Av (see question 38).

47.   What if a mourner completed his period of mourning during the three weeks?

Since he was unable to shave or have a haircut before the three weeks, he may do so until *Rosh Chodesh*.

48.   Is combing one's hair permitted?

This is permitted even during the week of Tisha b'Av.

49.   Is cutting one's nails permitted?

This is permitted until the week of Tisha b'Av. When Tisha b'Av is on Shabbos, it is permitted to cut one's nails on Friday in honor of Shabbos.

50.   May one recite the *b'racha shehecheyanu* for new fruits?

The prevalent custom is to refrain from reciting *shehecheyanu* on a weekday, but to permit its recital on a Shabbos or on *Rosh Chodesh*.

51.   May one eat a new fruit on a weekday without reciting *shehecheyanu*?

Ideally, a new fruit should not be eaten until Shabbos when *shehecheyanu* may be recited. If the fruit will not last until Shabbos, one may eat it on a weekday and recite *shehecheyanu*.

52.   May a pregnant woman or a sick person eat a new fruit on a weekday?

If such a person has a desire to eat a new fruit on a weekday, he may do so, but in this case the *b'racha shehecheyanu* should not be recited.

53. May one recite the *b'racha shehecheyanu* for new garments?

The prevalent custom is to refrain from reciting shehecheyanu on a weekday, but to permit its recital on a Shabbos before the nine days.

54. May one wear a new garment on a weekday without reciting *shehecheyanu*?

Ideally, such clothing should not be worn until Shabbos, when *shehecheyanu* may be recited. In extenuating circumstances, one may wear such clothing on a weekday until *Rosh Chodesh*, but the *b'racha shehecheyanu* should not be recited.

55. Is *shehecheyanu* recited at a *bris* or *pidyon haben*?

The *b'racha* is recited as usual for a *pidyon haben*, or for a *bris* (in *Eretz Yisroel*), even on Tisha b'Av.

56. Is *shehecheyanu* recited for a newborn girl?

Many parents have the custom to recite *shehecheyanu* when first seeing a newborn girl. The *b'racha* is recited as usual by both parents, even after *Rosh Chodesh*.

57. May one buy new clothes?

• Clothes of minor importance that do not require *shehecheyanu* (e.g. underwear, shoes, socks, shirts) may be bought and worn until *Rosh Chodesh*.

• Clothes of major importance that require *shehecheyanu* (e.g. jackets, suits, coats) may be bought until *Rosh Chodesh* according to most opinions, but it is preferable to refrain. (Regarding wearing them, see question 53.) According to some opinions, one may not buy such clothes.

58.   May one buy a new *tallis*?

A *tallis* is an important garment that requires the *b'racha shehecheyanu* (see previous question). One may buy a *tallis koton* even during the nine days if one has no other to wear, since this is a mitzvah item that does not require *shehecheyanu*.

59.   May one buy a new car, furniture, etc.?

•   If another person will also benefit from the item (e.g. a spouse or child), one may buy it until *Rosh Chodesh*. The *b'racha hatov vehameitiv* should be recited.

•   If only the purchaser will benefit from the item, one should ideally postpone buying it until after Tisha b'Av, in order to avoid reciting the *b'racha shehecheyanu* during the three weeks.

•   If he requires the item for his livelihood, he may purchase it, but the *b'racha shehecheyanu* should not to be said until after Tisha b'Av (if he still feels considerable joy from the item).

60.   May one buy a house?

The custom is to refrain from buying a house during the three weeks, since it is not a time of good fortune. If a person is forced to move out of his home, he may buy or rent a house even after *Rosh Chodesh*.

61.   May one look for a house?

This is permitted, but a written agreement should not be signed. If one is afraid that someone else may buy or rent the house before him, he may sign an agreement even after *Rosh Chodesh*. Some opinions discourage looking for a house during the three weeks.

62.   May one paint or decorate a house?

Strictly speaking, this is permitted until *Rosh Chodesh*, but it is praiseworthy to refrain.

63.   Should one avoid potentially dangerous activities?

Yes. Since this a time of misfortune, one should be especially careful to avoid all dangers.

64.   What sort of activities should be avoided?

- Going to dangerous locations.
- Striking a child or student.
- Undergoing a major operation that can be postponed until after Tisha b'Av.
- Going on a flight that can be postponed until after Tisha b'Av.

65.   May one swim in the sea or a swimming pool?

Strictly speaking, this is permitted until *Rosh Chodesh*, even if it is one's first visit of the season. However, one must take care to avoid deep or dangerous waters. Some opinions recommend not entering the sea.

Chapter Four

The Nine Days

66. When do the laws of the nine days commence?

At nightfall on the eve of *Rosh Chodesh* Av. According to some opinions, the laws commence at sunset.

67. What is forbidden during the nine days?

All forms of rejoicing are forbidden. One must also refrain from certain activities as a sign of mourning. The main restrictions are:

- Making improvements to one's home or garden.
- Laundering.
- Wearing new or laundered clothing.
- Making or buying new clothes.
- Eating meat or drinking wine.
- Bathing for pleasure.

Whoever refrains from rejoicing during the first ten days of Av will merit to witness ten miraculous changes that will occur at the end of days.

68. Which types of improvements to one's home are forbidden?

It is forbidden to do any building or construction work that is unnecessary for basic dwelling. For example, one may not build a vacation home or an extension to one's home. It is also forbidden to paint or decorate the home, or replace curtains, cabinets etc.

69.   May such work be done by a gentile?

• From *Rosh Chodesh*, a gentile may not be called to do such work.

• If an agreement was made with a gentile before *Rosh Chodesh*, the work may be done during the nine days. However, one should try to postpone the work until after Tisha b'Av, and should offer the gentile a small sum of money as compensation if necessary.

70.   May such work be done for a gentile?

A Jewish builder or painter is permitted to work as usual for gentile customers.

71.   May one build a shul?

A shul, *mikveh*, or yeshiva may be built and decorated during the nine days, since such work is a mitzvah.

72.   May one make repairs to a house?

All repairs and basic upkeep of the house are permitted. If walls have been damaged by mold or dampness, they may be repaired but not painted.

73.   May one clean the house as usual?

Yes. Some have the custom not to wash the floors except when it is really necessary and on *erev* Shabbos. The floor should not be polished.

74.   Which type of gardening is forbidden?

One may not plant anything for pleasure, such as trees, flowers, or grass. Regular upkeep of the garden such as weeding, watering, and mowing the lawn is permitted.

Chapter Five

Laundering during the Nine Days

75. What is included in the prohibition of laundering?

Adults' clothing may not be laundered or dry-cleaned, even if the clothing will not be worn until after Tisha b'Av. Towels, dishcloths, sheets, and tablecloths may also not be laundered.

76. When is the latest time to do laundry?

One may put a wash into the machine on *erev Rosh Chodesh* afternoon, provided that it will be finished before nightfall.

77. May one give laundry to a gentile cleaner?

• During the nine days one may not give clothes to a gentile to clean.

• Before *Rosh Chodesh* one may give them to a gentile, even if the clothes will be cleaned during the nine days.

78. May one wash the clothes of a gentile?

• This is permitted until the week of Tisha b'Av.

• During the week of Tisha b'Av, this is permitted if done in private. The clothes may not be washed in public, unless one's livelihood will suffer severely.

79.   May one wash children's clothes?

• Clothes of children who constantly soil themselves may be washed during the nine days. This is approximately until the age of five or six.

• Clothes of older children (until bar/bas mitzvah) may be washed until the week of Tisha b'Av, if necessary.

80.   May one wash adults' clothes together with children's?

No. Even when using a washing machine, one may not include adults' clothes with children's clothes.

81.   Are there any situations when adults' clothes may be washed?

• A woman who is required to wear white during the seven clean days may wash her clothes and sheets if necessary.

• A person who does not have clean clothes to wear on the Shabbos before Tisha b'Av may wash what is required on Thursday or Friday.

• A person who has only one garment (of a particular type) may wash this garment when necessary until the week of Tisha b'Av. The same applies to a person who has many garments but they are all dirty. According to some opinions, such clothes may be washed in hot water without detergent, even during the week of Tisha b'Av.

82.   May such clothes be hung outside to dry?

No, since this may arouse suspicion that one has done something wrong. The wet clothes should be hung indoors or dried in a machine.

83.   May children's laundry be hung outside to dry?

This is permitted. Since they are easily recognizable as children's clothes, one will not be suspected of doing something wrong.

84.   May one spot clean a stain on clothing?

- If the stain is noticeable, one may clean it.
- If the stain is not noticeable, one may not clean it thoroughly, but one may rub it with a damp cloth. If the stain will become permanent if not cleaned immediately, one may clean it.

85.   May one spot clean a tablecloth?

Only if the stain will become permanent if not cleaned immediately, or if one has no other tablecloth.

86.   What if a child soils his sheets?

One may wash the sheets.

87.   May a woman wash a *shaitel*?

A *shaitel* is an item of clothing and may not be professionally set. If it is dirty and she does not have a clean one to wear, it may be washed until the week of Tisha b'Av. It is permitted to comb or brush a *shaitel*.

88.   May one brush dusty clothes?

Yes. This includes a hat and shoes.

89.   May one polish shoes?

There are different customs about this. One may polish shoes in honor of Shabbos.

90.   May one do ironing?

Ironing is forbidden during the nine days. This includes Shabbos clothes.

91.   Why is it forbidden to wear new or laundered clothing?

A person who has lost a close relative may not wear laundered clothes for thirty days. In a similar vein, it is forbidden to wear laundered clothes during the nine days as a sign of mourning. One may certainly not wear any new clothes during the nine days.

92.   Must one wear dirty clothes for nine days?

No. Although it is forbidden to wear freshly laundered clothes, one may wear clothes that have already been worn for a short time. Therefore, a person should prepare the clothes that he wishes to wear during the nine days, by wearing them for a short time before *Rosh Chodesh*.

93.   For how long must the clothes be worn?

Until the feeling of freshness has been lost. This is after approximately half-an-hour under normal conditions.

94. May one iron the clothes after wearing them for a short time?

No, since this restores the freshness.

95. Must one prepare Shabbos clothes before *Rosh Chodesh*?

No. The main custom is to permit wearing freshly cleaned clothes in honor of Shabbos.

96. May one wear new clothes on Shabbos?

• New clothes of major importance may not be worn.

• New clothes of minor importance (e.g. underwear, socks, shirts) may not be worn, unless one has nothing clean to wear.

97. Must one prepare underwear before *Rosh Chodesh*?

There are different customs about this. It is praiseworthy for a person to be strict in this matter, and prepare even these clothes beforehand. A person who feels sensitive about this may be lenient to wear such clothes even if they are freshly laundered, but only when necessary. This includes underwear, socks, and pajamas.

98. Must children prepare their clothes for the nine days?

Children from the age of nine should not wear freshly laundered clothes during the week of Tisha b'Av, and should prepare them beforehand.

99.   What if one forgot to prepare clothes before *Rosh Chodesh*?

He should place them on a dirty or dusty floor to remove their freshness. If the floor is clean, he should tread on them to crease them. Alternatively, he may put them in the laundry hamper with dirty clothes for a short time.

100. May one prepare clothes by wearing them on Shabbos?

Since it is forbidden to prepare anything on Shabbos for the weekday, one may not wear fresh clothes on Shabbos specifically for this purpose. However, if one needs to undress on Shabbos, he may use the opportunity to wear different clothes when dressing again. Therefore, when dressing on Shabbos morning, one may wear fresh clothes, and save the clothes worn on Friday night for the following weekdays. The same applies if one goes to sleep during the day of Shabbos.

101. May one wear Shabbos clothes on a weekday?

No. Even if the Shabbos clothes are not freshly laundered, they may not be worn on a weekday.

102. From what time on *erev* Shabbos may one change into Shabbos clothes?

From *mincha ketana*. According to some opinions, one may change for Shabbos at whatever time one usually does.

103. Must one change into weekday clothes on *motzai* Shabbos?

According to some opinions, one should change into weekday clothes after *havdalah*. Other opinions say that this is unnecessary, and one may remain in Shabbos clothes until bedtime.

104. May one wear Shabbos clothes in honor of a *bris*?

The parents of the child, the *sandek*, the *mohel*, and the woman who carries in the baby may wear Shabbos clothes. According to some opinions, the grandparents of the child are also included. They should all change back into weekday clothes as soon as possible after the *bris*.

105. May one wear Shabbos clothes in honor of a *pidyon haben*?

The parents of the child and the *Cohen* may wear Shabbos clothes.

106. May one wear Shabbos clothes in honor of a bar mitzvah?

The parents and the boy may wear Shabbos clothes if the celebration is held on his birthday. Since one may not wear new clothes during the nine days, the boy must remember to wear his clothes for a short time before *Rosh Chodesh*. Clothes that require the *b'racha shehecheyanu* should be worn before the three weeks or on a Shabbos before *Rosh Chodesh* (see question 53).

107. May one wear Shabbos clothes when going on a date?

Yes.

108. May a woman wear jewelry during the nine days?

Yes.

109. May one use fresh bed linen?

It is forbidden to change the bed linen during the nine days, even in honor of Shabbos. Therefore, one should change the linen two days before *Rosh Chodesh*, in order to use them before the nine days. A woman may change her sheets at the start of the seven clean days.

110. May one provide clean bed linen for visitors?

Yes. Similarly, a hotel is permitted to change the linen for guests who arrive during the nine days. Nevertheless, a person who is staying at a hotel for several days must request that his sheets should not be changed until after Tisha b'Av.

111. May one use fresh towels?

Freshly laundered hand towels and bath towels may not be used during the nine days. Therefore, one should prepare several towels before *Rosh Chodesh* by using them at least once after they have been laundered. If all the prepared towels became completely soiled during the nine days, it is permitted to use a fresh one. Also, a fresh hand towel may be used on Shabbos.

112.   May one use a fresh tablecloth?

A freshly laundered tablecloth may not be used unless the tablecloth becomes completely soiled. A fresh tablecloth may be used on Shabbos.

Chapter Six

Making and Buying Clothes during the Nine Days

113. What is included in the prohibition of making clothes?

• One may not make any new clothes whether by sewing, weaving, knitting, or any other method. This is forbidden even if the garment will not be completed until after Tisha b'Av.

• One may not do embroidery or other needlework on clothing, tablecloths, etc.

• It is permitted to cut pieces of cloth in preparation for sewing after Tisha b'Av.

114. Does this also apply to a professional tailor?

The custom is to permit a tailor to continue earning a livelihood by making clothes for others. If possible, he should refrain during the week of Tisha b'Av, unless it is well known that he is doing work for gentiles.

115. May one make wedding clothes for a *chosson* or *kallah*?

It is permitted if there is not sufficient time to do this after Tisha b'Av.

116.   May a girl learn to sew?

• This is permitted if cancellation of a class will cause financial loss to the teacher. If possible, classes should not be held during the week of Tisha b'Av.

• It is forbidden to practice making clothes at home, unless the cloth will be discarded.

117.   May one repair garments?

• Simple repairs are permitted when necessary, e.g. sewing a tear, adding a patch, sewing on a button.

• According to most opinions, it is permitted to shorten or lengthen a garment.

118.   May one instruct a gentile to make or alter a garment?

This is permitted if the garment will not be ready until after Tisha b'Av. Nevertheless, it is praiseworthy to refrain from doing so.

119.   May shoes be repaired?

Yes. Even professional shoe repairs are permitted.

120.   May one tie tzitzis on a garment?

Yes.

121.   Which types of clothing may not be purchased?

It is forbidden to purchase all types of clothing, including those that do not require the *b'racha shehecheyanu*, e.g. shoes, socks, underwear. This applies even if one does not intend to wear them until after Tisha b'Av.

122. May one buy second-hand clothes?

This is forbidden if such clothes will give pleasure.

123. May a *chosson* or *kallah* buy clothes for their wedding?

This is permitted if they will not be able to buy them after Tisha b'Av.

124. May one buy a new *tallis*?

No. One may buy a *tallis koton* even during the nine days, if one has no other to wear.

125. May one buy bed linen, towels, etc.?

No.

126. What if there is a special sale during the nine days?

One may buy items at such a sale, if there is a considerable saving and one will not find them again at this price after Tisha b'Av. (See also questions 91, 109, and 111).

127. What if one has no suitable footwear for Tisha b'Av?

Since it is forbidden to wear leather shoes on Tisha b'Av (see question 236) one must remember to buy suitable footwear before *Rosh Chodesh*. If a person forgot to do so, he may buy simple cheap footwear during the nine days.

128. May one buy clothes for children?

No.

129. May one buy and/or give gifts?

• It is permitted to buy and give inexpensive gifts, e.g. on the occasion of a *bris* or bar mitzvah.

• It is forbidden to buy or give expensive gifts that will give considerable joy, e.g. an engagement ring.

• Clothes may not be bought even as a gift, e.g. for a newborn baby. If they were bought before the nine days, they may be given during the nine days.

130. May one buy new furniture and appliances, e.g. fridge, stove, etc.?

It is usually forbidden to buy important items during the nine days, since they bring a person much pleasure. If the old item broke during the nine days and cannot be repaired, a new one may be bought if needed urgently (see also question 59).

131. May one buy small household items?

It is permitted to buy items of minor importance that are needed regularly in the home, e.g. pots, pans, plates, etc.

132. May one buy *sefarim*?

One may buy *sefarim* that are needed for Torah study during the nine days.

Chapter Seven

Eating Meat and Drinking Wine during the Nine Days

133. Why is it forbidden to eat meat during the nine days?

- Eating meat gives a person pleasure.
- In order to remember the animal sacrifices that have ceased due to the destruction of the Temple.

134. Is poultry also forbidden?

Yes.

135. May one eat food that was cooked together with meat or poultry?

No.

136. May one eat food that was cooked in a clean *fleishig* pot?

This is permitted, even if the pot was used for meat in the last twenty-four hours.

137. May children eat meat?

- Until the age of three, children should not be restricted at all.
- For children between the ages of three and six, opinions differ whether they should be restricted.

According to some opinions, they may eat poultry but not meat.

• From the age of six, children should not eat meat or poultry.

• A child who is frail and would benefit from eating meat does not need to be restricted, irrespective of his age.

138. May a sick or weak person eat meat?

• A sick or weak person may eat meat.

• A healthy person who has a limited diet and is unable to eat dairy foods may eat poultry, or preserved meat that is at least three days old. If possible, he should refrain from eating this from the seventh of Av.

139. May a pregnant or nursing woman eat meat?

• A pregnant woman may eat poultry, or preserved meat that is at least three days old. If possible, she should refrain from eating this from the seventh of Av.

• A woman who has given birth may eat meat during the first thirty days following the birth. She should refrain from the seventh of Av, unless she isn't feeling well.

• A nursing mother may eat meat if she feels that refraining will be detrimental to her milk.

140. May one eat meat on Shabbos?

It is a mitzvah to eat meat on Shabbos, even during the nine days. If a person accepts Shabbos early on Friday afternoon, he may eat meat even before sunset. Similarly, if he is eating meat at *seuda shlishis*, he may continue even after nightfall.

141. May children be served their *fleishig* Shabbos meal on Friday afternoon?

Children who are not yet accustomed to wait until night for their Shabbos meal may be served meat one or two hours before Shabbos (see also question 137).

142. May one taste the *fleishig* Shabbos food on Friday?

It is a mitzvah to taste the Shabbos food every Friday afternoon to ascertain whether it is well flavored. However, during the nine days, the food may not be swallowed but should be spat out. (A *b'racha* should not be recited over such tasting.)

143. May one eat leftover *fleishig* foods at *melaveh malka*?

No.

144. May one eat meat on *Rosh Chodesh* Av?

No (unless it is Shabbos).

145. May one eat meat at a *seudas* mitzvah?

It is permitted to eat meat in honor of the mitzvah. This includes a *bris, pidyon haben, siyum,* and bar mitzvah on the boy's birthday.

146. May one invite any number of guests to such a meal?

• Before the week of Tisha b'Av, it is permitted to invite whoever one would normally invite to such a celebration. This includes relatives and friends.

• During the week of Tisha b'Av, only ten men may eat meat, besides the celebrant and his close family. Other guests may participate in the meal, but they must refrain from eating meat.

• If the *simcha* occurs on *erev* Tisha b'Av, the meal must begin before *halachic* midday.

147. On completion of which volumes may one make a siyum?

A *siyum* may be made on completion of any one of the following:

• A tractate of Talmud *Bavli* or Talmud *Yerushalmi*.

• One of the six orders of the Mishnah.

• One of the books of the prophets studied in depth.

• One of the four volumes of the *Shulchan Aruch*.

148. May one deliberately hurry or delay the completion of a volume in order to make a *siyum* during the nine days?

Meat may be served at a *siyum* only if the volume was studied at the usual pace, and the completion happened to occur during the nine days. If the completion was hurried or delayed, a *siyum* may be made but meat may not be served. If a person does not usually celebrate a *siyum* with a meal, he should preferably not serve meat at a *siyum* during the nine days.

149. What if a person recited a *b'racha* on meat during the nine days, and realized his mistake before eating it?

He should eat a minute amount of the meat in order not to recite a *b'racha* in vain.

150. May one eat parve sausages etc., which look like meat?

This is permitted, since people are accustomed to seeing such foods and will not suspect him of eating meat.

151. May a store sell meat to Jews during the nine days?

This is permitted since one may buy meat for Shabbos, for a *seudas* mitzvah, for sick people, or for after the nine days.

152. Why is it forbidden to drink wine during the nine days?

• Drinking wine gives a person much joy.
• In order to remember the wine libations that have ceased due to the destruction of the Temple.

153. Is grape juice also forbidden?

Yes.

154. May wine vinegar be used?

This may be used, since people do not drink it due to its sour taste.

155. Are other alcoholic drinks forbidden?

- If the drink does not contain any wine it is permitted.
- If the drink contains wine, it is permitted only if the taste of wine cannot be detected.
- According to some opinions, one should refrain from all alcoholic drinks except for a mitzvah or health reasons, since they give a person much joy.

156. May one eat cooked or baked foods that contain wine?

Although the wine enhances the taste of the food, this is permitted, provided that one cannot detect the actual taste of wine. According to some opinions, one should not add any wine when cooking, in case he inadvertently drinks some of the wine.

157. May one drink wine on Shabbos?

Yes. Therefore, wine or grape juice may be used for kiddush as usual, and may be served during the meals.

158. May one drink the wine of *havdalah*?

There are different customs about this:

- According to some opinions, the wine should be given to a child between the ages of six and nine. If such a child is not available, the person reciting *havdalah* should drink the wine himself.

- According to other opinions, the person reciting *havdalah* should drink the wine himself.

159. How much wine should be drunk?

One should drink the majority of a *reviyis*. If possible, one should drink a complete *reviyis* in order to recite an after-*b'racha*.

160. Should one use grape juice for *havdalah* rather than wine?

According to some opinions, this is preferable. Indeed, according to these opinions, one is not required to give the cup to a child when using grape juice.

161. Should one use beer for *havdalah* rather than wine or grape juice?

No. One may not use beer when wine and grape juice are easily obtainable.

162. May one drink wine on *Rosh Chodesh Av?*

No (unless it is Shabbos).

163. May one drink wine at a *seudas mitzvah?*

Yes (see question 145). This includes the wine used for *bensching*.

164. May one drink the wine used at the *bris* ceremony?

Although this wine is used in honor of the mitzvah, the custom is to give it to a child aged six or above, or to the mother of the baby if she is present. The child or mother should listen to the *b'racha* that is recited over the wine, and not speak until he/she drinks it. If neither is available, the person reciting the *b'racha* should drink the wine himself.

165. What if a person recited a *b'racha* over wine or grape juice and realized his mistake before drinking it?

He should drink a minute amount in order not to recite a *b'racha* in vain.

Chapter Eight

Bathing during the Nine Days

166. What is included in the prohibition of bathing?

It is forbidden to bathe or wash oneself for pleasure, but permitted for basic cleanliness. Therefore, under normal circumstances, one may not wash any part of the body with hot water, and may wash only the hands, face, and feet with cold water without soap.

167. What if part of one's body is dirty or perspired?

He may wash the affected area(s). Hot water or soap should not be used unless the dirt or perspiration cannot be removed otherwise.

168. What if one's entire body is perspired?

• According to most opinions, he may take a cold shower if he feels this is required for basic cleanliness. Soap should not be used unless necessary.

• According to some opinions, there is an additional limitation that he may not wash the entire body at once, but should wash one area at a time.

• According to some opinions, only a very sensitive person may take a shower, and each individual should use his judgment before being lenient in this matter.

169.   May one bathe children?

They may be bathed as frequently as necessary for basic cleanliness.

170.   May one shampoo the hair?

This is permitted if:

- he has a scalp condition that causes irritation, or
- his hair is full of perspiration, or
- he is a very sensitive person.

171.   May one bathe on *erev* Shabbos?

- According to most opinions, one may wash only the hands, face, feet, and hair with hot water without soap.
- According to some opinions, one may bathe as usual, especially in hot countries where people are accustomed to bathe more frequently.
- When *Rosh Chodesh* Av is on Friday, one may bathe the entire body with hot water and soap. When the eighth of Av is on Friday, one should bathe before *halachic* midday, if possible.

172.   May one bathe for medical reasons?

This is permitted, since it is not for pleasure. Therefore, a weak or sick person who is advised by a doctor to bathe in hot water or hot springs may do so. Similarly, a pregnant woman may bathe in hot water during the ninth month, if she believes that this is beneficial to her health.

173. How should a woman prepare herself for the *mikveh*?

• She should wash herself and immerse in the *mikveh* as usual. Similarly, she may wash herself as usual before the seven clean days.

• If the immersion will be on *motzai* Tisha b'Av, the custom is to make all the preparations after the fast, unless the fast finishes late.

174. May a man immerse in a *mikveh*?

• A man who is accustomed to immerse himself every *erev* Shabbos may do so on *erev* Shabbos in the nine days. If he occasionally does not go due to cold weather or lack of time, he may not go during the nine days.

• A man who immerses daily before *shacharis* or whenever he is *tamei* may do so.

• If possible, he should immerse only in a cold or lukewarm *mikveh*. If he is sensitive and cannot tolerate such a cold temperature, or if no such *mikveh* is available, he may immerse in a hot *mikveh*. However, in this case, he should not remain in the *mikveh* longer than is necessary, but should immerse and leave immediately.

175. Is swimming permitted during the nine days?

Swimming for pleasure or exercise is forbidden. Opinions differ regarding swimming for medical reasons, e.g. to provide relief from physical pains. If possible, one should use other forms of exercise.

176. What other activities should be avoided during the nine days?

Since the fortune of the Jewish people is not favorable during these days, one should try to avoid a lawsuit with a gentile until after Tisha b'Av. According to some opinions, the case should preferably be postponed until after the fifteenth of Av, and according to others until the month of Elul.

177. Is *kiddush levana* recited during the nine days?

The main custom is to wait until after Tisha b'Av, since *kiddush levana* should preferably be recited in a state of happiness (see also question 354). Some have a custom to recite it during the nine days in order to perform the mitzvah as soon as possible, or to avoid the risk of missing the opportunity entirely.

Chapter Nine
Erev Tisha b'Av

178. Is there any change to the prayers on *erev* Tisha b'Av?

Tachanun is omitted at *mincha*.

179. Do any restrictions of Tisha b'Av begin on *erev* Tisha b'Av?

After *halachic* midday, the following restrictions apply:

- One may not take pleasure walks.
- According to some opinions, one may learn only those topics of Torah that may be studied on Tisha b'Av (see question 249). Other opinions do not make such a restriction. It is praiseworthy to be strict if possible, but it is better to learn any topic of Torah than to waste one's time.

180. What is the *seuda hamafsekes*?

This is the final meal eaten before the fast commences. Since there are severe restrictions to this meal, the custom is to eat a regular meal early in the afternoon before *mincha*, and the *seuda hamafsekes* after *mincha*. One should take care not to overeat at the first meal, in order to be able to eat the *seuda hamafsekes*.

181. How is the *seuda hamafsekes* eaten?

The custom is to eat it while sitting on the ground, in order to feel grief over the destruction of the holy Temple. The mood should resemble that of a person who has just lost a close relative and is waiting for the funeral to begin.

182. Must one sit on the bare floor?

•   This is the most preferable position, but according to some opinions one should sit on a cloth or towel rather than on the bare floor.

•   A weak person who is unable to sit on the floor may sit on a pillow or a low chair.

•   If this is also too difficult, he may sit on a regular chair but in a different place in the room than usual.

183. Must one remove his shoes?

No, this is not required until sunset.

184. What should be eaten at this meal?

•   Bread should be eaten.

•   The custom is to eat only cold hard-boiled eggs and water, besides the bread.

•   If a person does not like eggs, he may eat lentils instead.

•   A piece of bread should be dipped in ashes, and one should say, "This is the meal of Tisha b'Av".

185. May one spread something on the bread?

The custom is to eat the bread plain. However, if a person wishes, he may spread cheese, butter, margarine, etc. on the bread.

186. May one eat any other foods?

• The custom is to eat only eggs or lentils, but if a person wishes he may eat a different cooked food.

• It is forbidden to eat more than one cooked food.

• One may eat any raw fruits and vegetables, but it is proper to refrain in order that the meal be simple and humble.

187. May one have any drinks?

• If possible, one should drink only water.

• It is forbidden to drink beer, unless one feels weak.

• It is forbidden to have any other alcoholic drink.

• The custom is to permit tea or coffee.

• One should not have soft drinks such as orange juice, cola, etc.

188. Should *zimun* be recited if three men are present?

No. If possible, the men should sit apart from one another during the meal. Nevertheless, even if they sit together, *zimun* is not recited.

189. May one eat or drink after *bensching*?

It is permitted to eat or drink again until sunset, unless one had firm intention not to do so. It is preferable to say or think before *bensching* that one is not accepting the fast until sunset.

190. May one sit on a regular chair after *bensching*?

This is permitted until sunset.

Chapter Ten
Fasting on Tisha b'Av

191. What is forbidden on Tisha b'Av?

The day of Tisha b'Av is unique in its restrictions, combining two sets of prohibitions. Firstly, it is a public fast with laws comparable to Yom Kippur. Secondly, it is a day of mourning with laws comparable to those of *shiva*. There are five prohibitions similar to Yom Kippur:

- Eating and drinking.
- Bathing.
- Applying oils.
- Wearing shoes.
- Marital relations.

In addition, there are four prohibitions similar to *shiva*:

- Learning Torah.
- Greeting people.
- Working.
- Sitting on a chair.

192. Why is Tisha b'Av a day of such severe mourning?

Five major tragedies happened to the Jewish nation on Tisha b'Av:

- It was decreed upon the generation of the wilderness that they would not enter *Eretz Yisroel*.
- The first holy Temple was destroyed.
- The second holy Temple was destroyed.

- The great city of Beitar was captured by the Romans, and tens of thousands of Jews were slain.
- The wicked Turnus Rufus plowed the site of the Temple and the surrounding area.

Following the episode of the spies, Hashem condemned this day to become destined for national disasters throughout history. When the Jewish nation wept in vain over the slanderous words of the spies, Hashem said, "You wept for no reason. I will establish this day as a time of weeping for all generations".

This sentence has been fulfilled countless times over, with the bloodstained annals of history bearing witness to the execution of this bitter decree. The infamous expulsion of the Jews from Spain took place on Tisha b'Av 1492, and in more recent times World War I broke out on Tisha b'Av 1914. On this day, the Jewish nation mourns over its long exile and yearns for the building of the third holy Temple, speedily in our days.

193. Do women need to fast?

Girls over bas mitzvah and women are obligated to fast if they are well, even if they find fasting difficult. Although certain communities are lenient regarding other fast days, all are strict on Tisha b'Av.

194. Should children be trained to fast?

No, children below bar/bas mitzvah do not need to fast, even for a few hours. Nevertheless, if they understand that it is a day of mourning, they should be given only simple foods and certainly not treats.

195. Is a pregnant woman required to fast?

• If she is strong and healthy, she should fast. It is recommended that she should drink large amounts of liquid in the days leading up to the fast, and rest as much as possible during the fast in order to preserve her strength. Wherever possible, conditions in the home should be arranged to ease fasting, e.g. using fans or air conditioning.

• If she is weak or is suffering from medical problems, she should not fast.

• If there is a fear that fasting may cause a miscarriage ו"ח, she should not fast.

• When the fast is postponed to the tenth of Av, a pregnant woman who has difficulty fasting is not required to fast all day.

• See also questions 198, 202 and 208.

196. Is a woman who has recently given birth required to fast?

• For the first seven days following the birth, she is forbidden to fast.

• Between seven and thirty days following the birth, she is not required to fast.

• After thirty days, she must fast unless there is a complication (see also question 200).

197. Between seven and thirty days, may she attempt to fast?

• According to some opinions, she should not attempt to fast the entire day, but should fast for a few hours.

- According to some opinions, the custom is to try to fast the entire day if she has completely recuperated from childbirth. If she feels weak during the fast, she should eat immediately.

198. Should such a woman begin to fast at night or only in the morning?

She should begin to fast at night like everyone else, and continue in the morning as long as she is able to (see also question 208).

199. What if a woman had a miscarriage ו"ח?

If the pregnancy lasted at least forty days, she should follow the same rules as for a regular birth.

200. Is a nursing mother required to fast?

- If fasting will not adversely affect her milk, she is required to fast.
- If she is feeling very weak or is suffering from medical problems, she should consult a doctor and a rav.
- When the fast is postponed to the tenth of Av, she is not required to fast all day if this is difficult (see also questions 198 and 208).

201. What if fasting will adversely affect her milk?

- If the baby is completely dependent on her milk and her fasting will cause a shortage or deterioration to the milk, she is not required to fast. However, she should preferably eat or drink only small quantities.

- Even if the baby is able to drink a milk formula as a temporary substitute, some opinions do not require her to fast and she may eat or drink as in the previous case. According to other opinions she should fast, unless she fears that this will cause her milk to cease.
- If the baby's principal diet is cereal or other foods, she must fast even if she is supplementing the diet by nursing.

202. What are the measurements of small quantities?

- The maximum quantity of food that may be eaten at one session is 30ml (one fluid ounce). This measurement is a volume and not a weight, and is the same for all types of food. It is recommended to eat substantially filling foods such as fish (e.g. tuna, sardines), which are more satisfying than lighter foods of the same volume.
- The liquid quantity is a cheekful. For an average person this is approximately 40ml (1.3 fluid ounces) and for a smaller person this could be 30ml (1 fluid ounce). This quantity is the same for all liquids and it is recommended to drink fruit juice, which is satisfying and healthy.

203. How often may such a person eat small quantities?

Only as often as is necessary.

204. How much time must one wait between sessions?

One must wait nine minutes between the end of one session and the beginning of the next. It is permitted to eat and drink at the same session.

205. What if a person is not well?

• If he is suffering from a headache, cold, or other minor ailment, he is required to fast, unless the fast is postponed to the tenth of Av (see also question 198).

• If he is ill, he is not permitted to fast, even if fasting will not endanger his life. A person who is not sure about his physical condition and his ability to fast should consult a doctor and a rav.

206. Should an ill person limit himself to eating or drinking if either one is sufficient?

Yes.

207. Should an ill person limit himself to small quantities of food or drink?

No, he may eat or drink as much as necessary. If possible, he should fast at night and delay eating until the morning.

208. May an ill person eat as much as he likes?

No. In order to participate in the public fast day, he should limit himself to a sufficient amount of simple foods.

209. How should a person who is able to fast take medicine if required?

A person may swallow bitter or tasteless medicines in tablet, capsule or liquid form, but not if they are pleasant tasting. The medicine should be taken without water or with a bitter tasting liquid. (If the medicine will still be effective when mixed with water, this is a practical solution since such liquid is usually bitter tasting.) If these alternatives are not feasible, he may take the medicine with a small amount of water, if refraining from doing so will cause illness.

210. Is a person who is fasting permitted to taste food and spit it out?

No. It is forbidden to taste even the tiniest amount of food, even if he is certain that he will not swallow anything.

211. May the mouth be rinsed?

One may rinse the mouth only if a bad taste causes extreme discomfort. Only a small amount of liquid should be used while leaning forwards in order to minimize the chance of it being swallowed.

212. May the teeth be cleaned?

The teeth may be cleaned with a dry toothbrush.

213. If a person said a *b'racha* on food or drink and then realized that it is a fast day, what should he do?

He must say ברוך שם כבד מלכותו לעולם ועד and not eat or drink anything.

214. If a person accidentally ate or drank what should he do?

He must stop immediately and continue to fast for the rest of the day. He is not obligated to fast on another day but if he wishes to gain atonement for his mistake he may do so. If this is difficult he may give a reasonable sum of money to charity.

215. When the fast is on Sunday, should a person who is not fasting recite *havdalah* before eating?

See question 385.

216. Should a sick man wear *tefillin* before eating?

According to most opinions, if he eats in the morning he should not wear *tefillin*, but if he eats after *halachic* noon he should first wear *tefillin*. If he *davens mincha* later in the day, he should wear *tefillin* again.

Chapter Eleven

Bathing on Tisha b'Av

217. What are the basic rules about bathing?

It is forbidden to wash any part of the body for pleasure, whether in hot or cold water. Even to allow a single finger to become wet is forbidden since this gives pleasure.

218. What if part of the body is dirty?

It is permitted to wash off dirt with cold water, but one should be careful to wash only the affected area.

219. What if parts of the body feel very sweaty?

It is preferable not to wash off sweat since it is not considered as dirt. Rather, one should wipe the affected area with a dry or damp towel. If a person is very sensitive, he may wash the area with cold water.

220. How should a person wash his hands when awakening in the morning?

The hands should be washed to the knuckles only (i.e. to the end of the fingers), but one does not need to be concerned if some of the water splashes a little further. One should wash each hand three (or four) times as usual.

221. What if one's eyes are sticky when awakening?

The stickiness may be washed off (see question 218).

222. How should one wash the hands after using the bathroom?

One should wash only to the knuckles. It is sufficient to wash each hand once, but if a person is accustomed to wash each hand three times throughout the year, he may do so on Tisha b'Av.

223. What if a person touched his shoes or scratched his head?

He may wash only his fingertips.

224. What if he touched a part of the body that is usually covered?

He may wash only the affected hand to the knuckles.

225. How do *Cohanim* wash their hands before blessing the congregation?

They may wash the entire hand up to the wrist, since it is a mitzvah for them to wash the hands.

226. How should a child or other person wash if they are to eat bread?

Since this is a mitzvah, the entire hand is washed.

227. Are children required to keep the above restrictions of washing?

Yes. Wherever possible, children should be trained to follow the above laws, whether washing by themselves or being washed by their parents.

228. May a person allow his hands to become wet when washing food or dishes for a person who is eating?

This is permitted since it is not being done for pleasure. Hot water should not be used if possible.

229. May a bride wash her face?

This is permitted for the first thirty days following the wedding.

230. May a person wash his hands before *mincha*?

Since this is a mitzvah, he may wash his hands up to the knuckles.

231. May a woman wash herself before the beginning of the seven clean days?

She may wash herself the minimum that is necessary.

232. If a woman needs to immerse in a *mikveh* on *motzai* Tisha b'Av, when should she prepare herself?

See question 173.

Applying Oils

233. What are the basic rules of applying oils?

It is forbidden to apply oils or creams to any part of the body even in a small quantity. This is only forbidden when done for pleasure, but it is permitted for hygiene or medical purposes. Therefore, one may not use soaps, perfumes, cosmetics, creams, lipstick, etc. It is permitted to use deodorants, anti-perspirants, medicinal creams, and talcum powder in order to maintain personal hygiene.

234. May a bride use cosmetics during the first thirty days following the wedding?

According to most opinions, this is permitted. According to some opinions, it is forbidden, and it is only permitted for her to wash her face (see question 229).

235. May one smell spices or snuff?

This is forbidden, since a person must refrain from such a pleasure on Tisha b'Av.

Chapter Twelve

Wearing Shoes on Tisha b'Av

236. Which shoes are included in this prohibition?

Shoes made of leather.

237. What if only a small part of the shoe is made of leather?

This is also forbidden, whether the leather is found in the sole, the upper part of the shoe or just in the straps.

238. What if the shoes are imitation leather but look like real leather?

According to some opinions, this is also forbidden because of מראית עין - one may not do an act that gives the impression to others that a prohibition is being done.

239. May one wear comfortable sports shoes etc.?

According to some opinions, such shoes should not be worn. The reason why we do not wear leather shoes is as an affliction and a discomfort, and therefore such footwear is inappropriate. It is praiseworthy to try to follow this opinion and limit oneself to thin-soled shoes that do not offer such comfort.

240. May one place a leather insert or foot support into the shoe?

- If the insert is left in the shoe permanently, then it is considered part of the shoe and is forbidden.
- If the insert is sometimes removed, it may be used on Tisha b'Av.

241. What if one is required to wear leather shoes for medical reasons?

Strictly speaking this is permitted. However, since many synthetic materials are available, one should try to obtain an alternative to leather if possible.

242. Are children allowed to wear leather shoes?

Strictly speaking, children below bar/bas mitzvah are permitted to wear leather shoes. However, it is customary to train children to wear other footwear from the age of two or three.

243. What is included in the prohibition of marital relations?

In addition to marital relations, all physical contact between husband and wife is forbidden, and the laws of *niddah* separation should be followed. According to most opinions, these additional restrictions apply only at night, but according to some opinions, they apply also during the day.

Chapter Thirteen

Learning Torah on Tisha b'Av

244. Why is it forbidden to learn Torah?

The verse says, "The instructions of Hashem are upright, gladdening the heart" (Psalms 19:9). Therefore, one may study only the topics of Torah that deal with tragedies and mourning.

245. May one think about topics of Torah?

This is also forbidden, since one derives pleasure from it.

246. Do these restrictions also apply to women?

Yes.

247. May one study Torah with children?

- It is forbidden to teach them regular Torah topics.
- It is permitted to relate to them the story of the destruction of the Temples and similar stories of persecution and calamities.
- Opinions differ whether one may teach them other Tisha b'Av topics (see question 249).

248. May children study regular Torah topics by themselves?

• Children below the age of six do not need to be prevented from studying any topics by themselves.

• From the age of six, children should be trained to study only topics dealing with tragedies and mourning.

249. Which Torah topics may one study?

• The story of the destruction of the two Temples. This can be found in the Talmud, midrash, and similar works.

• The book of *Eicha* (Lamentations), its midrash, and commentaries.

• The book of *Iyov* (Job) and its commentaries.

• The sections of the book of Jeremiah that deal with tragedy and destruction, and the commentaries. One must omit the sections that deal with the destruction of other nations and with consolation.

• Stories of persecution and calamities that befell the Jewish nation throughout the ages, including the holocaust.

• The *kinnos*.

• The laws of Tisha b'Av.

• The laws of mourning.

• The third chapter of *Moed Koton* in the Talmud.

250. May one study the portions of the Torah that are read in shul on Tisha b'Av?

• The morning reading may be studied by everyone, since it deals with tragedy.

- The afternoon reading may not be studied, but the person who will read it in shul may prepare it beforehand.

251. May one study books of *mussar*?

- It is permitted and even praiseworthy to do so, if the intention is to arouse the heart to repentance and the mending of one's ways (see question 5).
- According to some opinions, one should avoid works that quote verses from *Tanach* or statements of the Sages.

252. May the permitted topics be studied in depth?

According to some opinions, they should only be studied on a simple level, since deep study brings a person joy. Some opinions permit studying in depth, since it is perfectly normal to search for answers to questions and difficulties that arise.

253. May one study these topics with a partner?

Yes.

254. May one record new Torah insights that arise during study?

This is forbidden, since the writing of Torah ideas brings joy. However, if a person is afraid that he may forget the insights, he may make a brief note of them, and rewrite them properly after Tisha b'Av.

255. Are men obligated to learn Torah on Tisha b'Av?

• According to most opinions, a man is obligated to study Torah on Tisha b'Av, except that he is limited to certain topics.

• According to some opinions, the mitzvah of learning Torah is suspended on Tisha b'Av, and the study of permitted topics is optional.

• Nevertheless, all opinions agree that one must not be distracted from the mood of mourning throughout the entire day. It is certainly forbidden to listen to the radio, read newspapers and magazines, books, etc., or to pass the time with frivolous conversation. This applies also to women.

256. May one say *tehillim*?

• *Tehillim* for a sick person may be said all day.

• *Tehillim* that are said on a daily basis may not be said in the morning. Preferably, one should also not say them in the afternoon.

257. Should one say the entire bedtime shema?

According to most opinions, this should be said as usual.

258. May one give a *halachic* ruling?

This is forbidden, unless the question is relevant to Tisha b'Av, e.g. for a sick person who requires an immediate reply. Explanations of the ruling should not be given.

Chapter Fourteen

Greeting People on Tisha b'Av

259. What is included in this prohibition?

- One may not greet another person on Tisha b'Av.
- One may not give or send a gift on Tisha b'Av.

260. Which greetings are forbidden?

One may not say "Shalom", "Good morning", and similar greetings.

261. May one respond to a greeting?

A person who is greeted may respond in a low tone, in order not to create offense. If possible, he should not respond but should explain to the other person that greetings are forbidden on Tisha b'Av.

262. How should one respond to a telephone call?

Instead of saying "hello", one should say "yes". One must remember that idle conversation is forbidden, and telephone calls should be made only for urgent needs. One may not conclude the call by saying "goodbye".

263. May one nod the head as a form of greeting?

No.

264. May one wish a person mazel-tov?

This is permitted, since it is a blessing rather than a greeting.

265. May one shake hands when wishing mazel-tov?

This is also permitted.

266. May one inquire of another how he is feeling?

Yes.

267. May a traveler inform his family that he has arrived safely?

Yes.

268. Which type of gift may not be given?

All gifts are forbidden, even on the occasion of a *bris*, etc.

269. May one give charity to the poor?

Yes. Indeed, it is a great mitzvah to give charity on a fast day (see question 6).

270. May one send food to a needy person for after the fast?

Yes.

Chapter Fifteen
Working on Tisha b'Av

271. Which type of work is forbidden?

• In the evening and in the day before *halachic* noon, one may not do any type of work that requires some time. Jobs that can be done in a short time are permitted.

• After *halachic* noon, all forms of work are permitted, but a person must not become engrossed in his activities, since one's mind should not be diverted from mourning.

• It is praiseworthy to refrain from time-consuming work during the entire day.

272. Is business permitted?

• One may buy or sell food even before noon.

• Other forms of business are permitted after noon, but only if they can be conducted in a short time. A pious individual should avoid all business activities.

• Whoever engages in work or business on Tisha b'Av and becomes distracted from the mourning will not see any blessing from such activities.

273. May work be done for a person by a gentile?

This is permitted even before noon. However, construction work or renovations are forbidden since this is too public.

274. May business be done through a gentile?

If possible, this should be avoided, unless refraining will cause financial hardship.

275. Is housework permitted?

Housework is permitted after *halachic* noon, e.g. preparing food, washing dishes, making beds, etc. It is praiseworthy to postpone housework until after the fast wherever possible.

276. May one wash the floor in the afternoon?

Although some have a custom to do this in anticipation of the arrival of *moshiach*, the widespread custom is to refrain.

Chapter Sixteen

Sitting on a Chair on Tisha b'Av

277. Why is it forbidden to sit on a chair?

A mourner during the week of *shiva* may not sit on a chair. On Tisha b'Av we are all mourners over the destruction of the Temple.

278. When does this restriction apply?

From the commencement of the fast until *halachic* noon on Tisha b'Av. After noon one may sit on a regular chair.

279. Must one sit directly on the floor?

• If possible, one should sit on the floor, but it is permitted to sit on a pillow or cushion. According to some opinions, one should not sit on the bare floor.

• If this is too difficult, one may sit on a low chair or stool.

280. How low should the chair be?

According to most opinions it should be less than twelve inches high (30cm). According to some opinions, one may use any chair that is lower than usual, irrespective of its height.

281.   What if this is also too difficult?

A person who is unable to sit on a low chair may sit on a regular chair. This includes sick or elderly people, and pregnant or nursing mothers.

282.   What if a person is traveling?

It is permitted to sit normally while traveling (e.g. in a car, bus, etc.). According to some opinions, it is praiseworthy to stand if possible.

283.   Must a person who is sitting on the floor stand up for a rav or elderly person?

Yes. This mitzvah applies even on Tisha b'Av.

284.   Is there any restriction about sleeping in bed?

A person should deprive himself of some comfort when sleeping on the night of Tisha b'Av. For example, if he usually uses two pillows, he should remove one. If he usually uses one pillow, he should sleep without it. Some have the custom to place the mattress on the floor, and some place a stone under the pillow or mattress.

285.   What if this is too difficult?

People who are weak and pregnant women are not required to make such changes. Similarly, if these changes will prevent a person from sleeping, he may sleep as usual.

286. Do these restrictions apply when sleeping during the day?

According to some opinions, yes.

287. Are there any other restrictions to pleasure?

A person should refrain from all pleasurable activities on Tisha b'Av. For example, one may not go for a stroll, read a newspaper, or listen to the radio.

Chapter Seventeen

Prayers on Tisha b'Av

288. Why is there a custom to remove the curtain from the Ark?

The verse in *Eicha* (2:17) says "בצע אמרתו" which means, "He carried out His decree". However, the midrash interprets the words to mean "He tore His royal garments", referring to the piercing of the curtain in the holy Temple by the Roman emperor Titus. As a symbol of this desecration, there is a custom to remove the curtain from the holy Ark.

289. When should the curtain be removed?

Before the commencement of *ma'ariv*. When Tisha b'Av is on *motzai* Shabbos, it should not be removed before the termination of Shabbos.

290. When should the curtain be returned?

Before the commencement of *mincha* on Tisha b'Av afternoon (see question 337).

291. Should anything else be removed?

Some have the custom to remove the coverings of the *bimah* and the chazan's pulpit.

292.   Are there any other changes to the shul?

The lighting is reduced. Only the minimum amount of lights should be used to enable people to *daven* without difficulty.

293.   Should the special lights by the chazan's pulpit be lit?

No. However, they are lit for *mincha*.

294.   Why is the lighting reduced?

One reason is based on the verse in *Eicha* (3:6), which says "He placed me in darkness". Another reason is based on the midrash, that at the time of the destruction, Hashem asked the angels what a king should do when mourning. When they replied that he extinguishes the lights, Hashem said "I will do the same", as it says "The sun and the moon became dark" (*Yoel* 2:10).

295.   Should the lighting also be reduced at home?

This is not necessary, but some have the custom to do so.

296.   May a mourner go to shul during the week of *shiva*?

• During the first three days of *shiva* he may go in the morning but not in the evening.

• After the first three days, he may go also in the evening.

297. How should one dress for shul?

One should wear plain weekday clothes as a sign of mourning. Men should not wear a tie and women should not wear jewelry. Some have a custom to wear old clothes that are torn or ragged.

298. Does this also apply when Tisha b'Av is on *motzai* Shabbos?

See question 375.

299. Is there any change to *ma'ariv*?

Ma'ariv is said as usual until the *kaddish* after *shemoneh esrei*. However, the prayers should be said slowly and in a quiet mournful voice.

300. May one sit on the chairs in the shul?

No. This is forbidden until Tisha b'Av afternoon (see question 278). During *ma'ariv* and *shacharis* one should sit on the floor or a low chair. If one prefers, he may stand during the prayers, but during the recital of *Eicha* and *kinnos* one should sit on the floor or a low chair as a sign of mourning.

301. May one sit on the stairs next to the Ark?

Yes.

302. What is said after *shemonei esrei*?

The book of *Eicha* is read by the chazan, and in some communities it is read from a scroll of parchment. Some have the custom that a *b'racha* is recited by the chazan before the reading (על מקרא מגילה) in which case the congregation should listen carefully to the *b'racha* .

303. Should the *b'racha* be recited while standing?

No, the chazan and the congregation should sit on the floor. (This is an exception to the rule, which usually requires one to stand for such a *b'racha*.)

304. Should the congregation recite *Eicha* together with the chazan?

• If it is read from parchment, the congregation should listen.

• If it is not read from parchment, the congregation may listen or recite it quietly with the chazan.

305. What if a person missed some words?

Nothing needs to be done.

306. How should *Eicha* be recited?

It should be recited in a low voice with the traditional mournful tone. One should pause briefly between one verse and the next. The last verse of each chapter should be read louder, and each succeeding chapter should be read slightly louder than the previous one.

307. How is *Eicha* concluded?

The verse *Hashiveinu* is recited aloud by the congregation and then by the chazan. The final verse is then recited quietly by the chazan. Finally, the verse

Hashiveinu is repeated aloud by the congregation and chazan.

308. What is said after *Eicha*?

A few *kinnos* are said by the congregation led by the chazan. The *ma'ariv* service is concluded with *ve'ata kadosh*, *kaddish* by the chazan without *tiskabeil*, and *aleinu*.

309. Why is *tiskabeil* omitted from *kaddish*?

The verse in *Eicha* (3:8) says "He shut out my prayer". It is therefore inappropriate to recite the line *tiskabeil*, which means "our prayers should be accepted". This is also omitted during *shacharis*, but recited at *mincha*.

310. Is *viyhi no'am* recited when Tisha b'Av is *motzai* Shabbos?

No. This verse was composed when the *mishkan* was erected, and it is inappropriate to say it on the day the Temples were destroyed.

311. Is *veyiten lecha* recited when Tisha b'Av is *motzai* Shabbos?

No, since it is not a time of blessing and joy. Similarly, those who have the custom to bless their children on *moztai* Shabbos should not do so on Tisha b'Av.

312. Are women required to go to shul?

Although there is no obligation, it is praiseworthy for them to go, in order to hear the recital of *Eicha*.

313. Should children be brought to shul?

Young children should not be brought, since they are prone to playing games and making noise. This greatly disturbs the serious atmosphere of mourning. Older children who can behave properly should be trained to participate in the service.

314. How should one leave shul?

If possible, people should go home on their own and not in groups. They should go silently, and certainly not engage in idle conversation.

315. Should *Eicha* and *kinnos* be recited by a person who must remain at home?

A person at home should try to recite them, if possible.

Shacharis

316. Are there any changes to the morning *brachos*?

- The *tallis* and *tefillin* are not worn.
- Opinions differ whether a *b'racha* should be recited over the *tallis koton*. It is therefore advisable to avoid the problem by continuing to wear the *tallis koton* while sleeping at night. In this case, the *b'racha* is definitely not recited.
- Some people have the custom to omit the *b'racha* שעשה לי כל צרכי since this refers to leather shoes, which may not be worn on Tisha b'Av. Those who follow this custom should recite the *b'racha* when putting on leather shoes after the fast. However, the

main custom is to recite the *b'racha* as usual in the morning.

317. Are all the sections of *korbanos* said?

It is permitted to say whichever sections one is accustomed to say during the year.

318. Should one kiss the tzitzis at the conclusion of *baruch she'amar*?

The main custom is not to kiss them, and this applies also when reciting the shema. Some have the custom not to wear the tzitzis out of their garment until the afternoon.

319. Are there any changes to *shemoneh esrei*?

• The quiet *shemoneh esrei* is said without change. During the repetition, the chazan adds the prayer *aneinu*.

• The chazan omits the paragraph containing the priestly blessing and the *Cohanim* do not bless the congregation.

320. What is the order of prayers after *shemoneh esrei*?

• *Avinu malkeinu* is not recited.
• *Tachanun* is omitted.
• The Torah is read (*Devarim* 4:25-40).
• The *haftarah* is read (Jeremiah 8:13-9:23).
• *Kinnos* are recited.

321.   May a mourner during *shiva* be called to the Torah?

Yes. He may also read the Torah.

322.   May a bar mitzva boy be called to the Torah?

He should be called up at *mincha* and not at *shacharis*. The father may then recite the *b'racha baruch shepetarani*.

323.   May a person recite the *b'racha hagomeil*?

He should recite it at *mincha* and not at *shacharis*.

324.   May a *mi shebeirach* be said?

- For a *simcha* (e.g. *bris*, birth) it may be said at *mincha* but not at *shacharis*.
- For a sick person it may be said at *shacharis*.

325.   May a person who was called to the Torah thank the *gabbai*?

No.

326.   May a person who has *yahrzeit* recite the prayer for the deceased (*Eil malei rachamim*)?

No.

327.   Should the person who lifts up the *sefer Torah* sit on a regular chair?

Yes.

328. How much time should be spent reciting the *kinnos*?

The *kinnos* should be recited slowly and mournfully, and certainly not rushed. If possible, the recital should continue until close to midday.

329. Are women obligated to say the *kinnos*?

Yes, if possible.

330. What if a person does not understand the *kinnos*?

The *kinnos* are recited in order to arouse feelings of mourning and grief over the destruction of the Temples, the persecutions suffered by the Jewish nation, and the pain caused to the Holy Shechinah. Therefore, there is little or no point in reciting the *kinnos* by rote. A person who does not understand them should use a translation, and recite the *kinnos* in a language with which he is familiar.

331. What if a person cannot keep up with the congregation?

He should say the *kinnos* slowly at his pace in a way that will arouse the appropriate emotions. There is no obligation to recite the entire *kinnos*.

332. May one leave shul during *kinnos* in order to take a break?

Except for an emergency, it is forbidden to leave shul during *kinnos*, since one must not divert his mind from the mourning. Similarly, it is forbidden to engage in conversation about any other subject.

333. May the *kinnos* be said while standing?

No, they should be said while sitting on the floor or on a low chair (see question 300). The custom is to arise before reciting the *kinnah Eli tziyon*.

334. What is the order of prayers after *kinnos*?

- *Ashrei* is said, followed by *uva le'tziyon*.
- *Lamnatzeach* is omitted. The second verse of *uva le'tziyon* (*va'ani zos*) is also omitted, unless there is a *bris* is shul.
- *Kaddish* is recited by the chazan, omitting *tiskabeil*.
- *Aleinu* is said.
- The psalm of the day and *pitum haketores* are omitted.

335. Should *Eicha* be recited after *shacharis*?

There is a widespread custom to do so. A *b'racha* should not be recited even if a scroll of parchment is used. If a person is unable to *daven* in shul, it is correct for him to say *Eicha* after *shacharis*.

336. May one say the six remembrances and the thirteen principles of faith?

A person who says them every day may say them at *mincha* but not after *shacharis*.

Mincha

337. Should the shul be re-organized before *mincha*?

Yes. The curtain should be returned to the Ark and the coverings to the *bimah* and chazan's pulpit. All the lights are lit, including the special lights by the chazan's pulpit.

338. May a mourner during *shiva* go to shul for *mincha*?

No. He should organize a *minyan* at home.

339. May one wash the hands before *mincha*?

It is correct to wash them up to the knuckles.

340. Are the *tallis* and *tefillin* worn at *mincha*?

Yes.

341. Are *brachos* recited over the *tallis* and *tefillin*?

Yes. When reciting the *b'racha* over the *tallis*, one should have in mind to include the *tallis koton*. A person who does not wear a *tallis* should ask someone who does to include him with his *b'racha*.

342. May one say the verses when putting on the *tallis* and *tefillin*?

Yes.

343. May one say the usual four paragraphs from the Torah while wearing the *tefillin*?

There are different customs about this.

344. Should anything be said before *mincha*?

• The psalm of the day and *pitum haketores* are said.

• *Korbanos* may be said by people who say them regularly at *mincha*.

345. What is the order of prayers?

• *Ashrei* is recited.
• The Torah and *haftarah* are read as on other fast days.
• *Shemoneh esrei* is recited.
• *Avinu malkeinu* is not recited.
• *Tachanun* is omitted.
• *Kaddish* is said by the chazan including *tiskabeil*.
• *Aleinu* is recited.

346. Are there any changes to *shemoneh esrei*?

• A special prayer *nacheim* is added in the *b'racha* of *veliyrushalayim*.

• *Aneinu* is added in the *b'racha* of *shema koleinu*. (The chazan adds it as a separate *b'racha* before *refa'einu*.)

• *Sim shalom* is said instead of *shalom rav*, even if one is not fasting, nor *davening* with a *minyan*.

- A special prayer is inserted before the end of *shemoneh esrei*. This begins רבון כל העולמים גלוי וידוע לפניך.

347. What if one forgot to say *nacheim*?

- He should insert it before *vesechezena eineinu*, but the special conclusion of *nacheim* should not be said.
- If he forgot to say it there, he should say it just before the verse *yihyu leratzon* at the end of *shemoneh esrei*.
- If he forgot to say it there, he does not repeat *shemoneh esrei*.

348. What if he forgot to say *aneinu*?

If he has already concluded the *b'racha* of *shema koleinu*, he should continue and say *aneinu* just before the verse *yihyu leratzon* at the end of *shemoneh esrei*. If he forgot to say it there also, *shemoneh esrei* is not repeated.

349. Should a person who is exempt from fasting say *nacheim*?

Yes.

350. May a person who is exempt from fasting say *aneinu*?

No, he should omit it. Similarly, he should omit the prayer רבון כל העולמים.

351. May one wear *tefillin* of *Rabbeinu Tam*?

A person who wears them throughout the year may wear them on Tisha b'Av (see also question 343).

352. When should one take off his *tefillin*?

Before *ma'ariv*. According to some opinions, *tefillin* should be taken off before sunset.

After Ma'ariv

353. Which laws apply after the fast?

• It is praiseworthy to wash the entire hand three times, since the hands were not washed fully in the morning.

• A person who did not say the *b'racha* שעשה לי כל צרכי in the morning (see question 316) should say it in the evening when putting on leather shoes.

• *Kiddush levana* is recited (see question 177).

• *Havdalah* is recited if the fast is on Sunday (see questions 394 and 395).

• The laws of the nine days continue (see chapter nineteen).

354. May one recite *kiddush levana* before eating?

It is preferable to put on leather shoes and eat before reciting *kiddush levana*. However, if by doing so one will not be able to say it with a *minyan*, he may say it immediately.

Chapter Eighteen

When Tisha b'Av falls on Shabbos or Sunday

355. What are the main changes when Tisha b'Av falls on Shabbos or Sunday?

When Tisha b'Av falls on Shabbos, the main changes are:

- The fast is postponed until Sunday.
- Bathing is permitted on *Rosh Chodesh* (see question 171).
- Marital relations are forbidden on Friday night.
- Washing any part of the body with hot water is forbidden on Shabbos.

When Tisha b'Av falls on Shabbos or Sunday, the main changes are:

- There is no special *seuda hamafsekes* before the fast.
- Some of the laws of Tisha b'Av begin only at nightfall on *motzai* Shabbos, instead of at sunset.
- *Havdalah* is postponed until Sunday night.

356. When Tisha b'Av falls on Shabbos and is postponed to Sunday, is the preceding week considered as the week in which Tisha b'Av occurs?

There are different opinions about this. Therefore:

- One should be strict about this concerning laundering and haircuts (see questions 38, 40, 41, 44, 46, 78, 79 and 81).
- One may be lenient about matters concerning meat and wine, cutting nails, and making clothes (see questions 33, 49, 114 and 146).

357. May a woman immerse in a *mikveh* on Friday night that is Tisha b'Av?

Yes. In this case, marital relations are permitted.

358. May a man immerse in a *mikveh* on Shabbos morning that is Tisha b'Av?

If he immerses every Shabbos morning or whenever he is *tamei*, he may immerse but only in a cold *mikveh*.

359. Are there any changes to the prayers in this situation?

- *Tzidkascha* is not said at *mincha*.
- *Pirkei Avos* is not said at *mincha*.

360. May one sing and throw treats when a *chosson* is called up to the Torah?

According to the prevalent custom, this is permitted. Some opinions recommend that this be done on the previous Shabbos.

361. May one hold a public kiddush on this Shabbos?

- If the kiddush can be held on a different Shabbos, it is preferable to defer it.

- If the kiddush cannot be held on a different Shabbos (e.g. for a *chosson*), it is permitted.

362. May one eat meat and drink wine at the Shabbos meals?

Yes. This is permitted even at *seuda shlishis*.

363. May one invite guests to the Shabbos meals?

Yes. However, one should not invite guests for *seuda shlishis* unless he does so regularly.

364. May one sing *zemiros* at the Shabbos meals?

Yes. This is permitted even at *seuda shlishis*.

365. May one go for a stroll on this Shabbos?

- When the ninth of Av is Sunday, one may not go for a stroll on Shabbos after *halachic* noon.
- When the ninth of Av is Shabbos, one may not go for a stroll at any time of the day.

366. May one visit family or friends?

No.

367. May one learn Torah on this Shabbos?

- Before *halachic* midday, it is permitted to learn Torah.
- After *halachic* midday, many opinions permit learning Torah. If a person can limit himself to the

topics that are permitted on Tisha b'Av, he is praiseworthy.

• It is permitted to recite the *sedra* and its *targum* all day.

368. May one take pills on Shabbos to alleviate the pains of fasting?

• It is permitted to take them on Shabbos until sunset only if they are mixed with a food or drink. One should preferably prepare the mixture before Shabbos.

• One may take them without water on *motzai* Shabbos unless they are pleasant tasting (see question 209).

369. May a communal *seuda shlishis* be held in shul?

No. Everyone should eat at home.

370. Are there any changes to *seuda shlishis*?

• Although any food may be served, including meat and wine, and *zemiros* may be sung, the mood should be somewhat subdued.

• A person should not say that he is eating in order to have strength to fast, but he may think this.

• One must stop eating and drinking before sunset, since the fast begins at this time. **People should be reminded about this, as it is unlike a regular Shabbos.**

371. Must one *bensch* before sunset?

It is permitted to *bensch* after sunset, but one should try to wash *mayim acharonim* before sunset, if possible.

372. May one *bensch* with a *zimun*?

Yes (compare question 188).

373. May one eat or drink after *seuda shlishis*?

If one *bensched* before sunset, one may eat or drink until sunset. It is not necessary to have this in mind when *bensching* (compare question 189).

374. Which prohibitions of Tisha b'Av commence at sunset?

All the prohibitions except wearing shoes and sitting on a chair commence at sunset. These two activities are permitted until nightfall.

375. When should one change one's shoes and Shabbos clothes?

There are two customs:

• Some go to shul before nightfall and begin *ma'ariv* at the usual time of *motzai* Shabbos. The chazan should say *baruch hamavdil bein kodesh lechol*, remove his shoes, and then say *barchu*. The congregation should respond to *barchu* and then remove their shoes. Care must be taken not to touch one's shoes when removing them. The Shabbos clothes are not removed until one returns home after *ma'ariv*. This is the prevalent custom in *chutz la'aretz*.

• Some shuls delay the commencement of *ma'ariv*, allowing people to remain at home until nightfall. At the time of *motzai* Shabbos everyone should say the phrase *baruch hamavdil bein kodesh lechol*, remove his shoes, and change into weekday clothes before *ma'ariv*. This is the prevalent custom in *Eretz Yisroel*.

376. According to the first custom, may one bring Tisha b'Av footwear to shul before *ma'ariv*?

Even if there is an *eiruv* this is forbidden, since one may not prepare on Shabbos for *motzai* Shabbos. It is also forbidden to change one's shoes before going to shul, since this is disgracing the Shabbos. It is therefore advisable to leave suitable footwear in shul before Shabbos to wear on *motzai* Shabbos.

377. If a person usually waits until the time of *Rabbeinu Tam*, when should he change his shoes and clothes?

The local custom should be followed.

378. Is the *b'racha* recited over the spices?

No. It is forbidden to smell spices on Tisha b'Av (see question 235).

379. Is the *b'racha* recited over a *havdalah* candle?

Yes. According to one custom, it is recited in shul before the reading of *Eicha*. According to another custom, it is recited at home before *ma'ariv*, if there is time. According to some opinions, the *b'racha* should be recited over two regular candles and not over a braided *havdalah* candle.

380. Is a woman obligated to recite this *b'racha*?

If possible, she should listen to the *b'racha* being recited by a man. If this is not possible, most opinions permit her to recite this *b'racha* herself.

381. What if a person forgot or missed this *b'racha* before *Eicha*?

He should recite it later in the evening.

382. Are there any changes to the *ma'ariv* service?

• The two chapters of *tehillim* customarily sung before *ma'ariv* are omitted.

• *Viyhi no'am* and *veyiten lecha* are omitted (see questions 310 and 311).

383. May a man fold his *tallis* on *motzai* Shabbos?

Yes.

384. May one wash the Shabbos dishes on *moztai* Shabbos?

No. They may not be washed until Tisha b'Av afternoon.

385. Should a person who is not fasting recite *havdalah* before eating?

Yes. However, if he only needs to drink water throughout the fast, he should not recite *havdalah*.

386. Should such a person recite *havdalah* immediately on *motzai* Shabbos or wait until he needs to eat?

He should wait until he needs to eat (see also question 198).

387. Which sections of *havdalah* are recited?

The introductory verses and the *b'racha* over spices should be omitted. The *b'racha* over a candle should be omitted if he already recited or heard it at the termination of Shabbos, or if he is reciting *havdalah* during the day.

388. Should *havdalah* be recited over wine, grape juice, or another drink?

• According to most opinions, beer is the most preferred drink.

• If this is not possible, some opinions prefer the use of a drink that has national importance. (A rav should be consulted to ascertain which drinks qualify for this purpose.) Other opinions question the use of such drinks, and prefer the use of grape juice.

- If nothing else is available, wine may be used.

389. If wine or grape juice is used, should the cup be given to a child to drink?

- If a child above the age of six is available, the cup should be given to him.
- If not, the person who recites *havdalah* should drink the cup himself.

390. How much of the cup should be drunk?

A cheekful only.

391. May other members of the family fulfill the mitzvah by listening to this *havdalah*?

If *havdalah* is being recited by a man, they may fulfill their obligation this way and will not be required to recite *havdalah* after the fast.

392. Are children obligated to recite *havdalah* before they eat?

According to most opinions, they do not recite *havdalah* before eating.

393. After the fast may one eat or drink before *havdalah*?

With the exception of water, it is forbidden to eat or drink anything before *havdalah*. This also applies to women.

394. Which drink should be used for *havdalah*?

One should use wine or grape juice. The person who recites *havdalah* should drink the cup himself (compare question 158).

395. Which parts of *havdalah* are recited?

Only the two *brachos borei p'ri hagafen* and *hamavdil*. The introductory verses are omitted, as are the *brachos* over the spices and candle.

396. What if he forgot to recite the *b'racha* over a candle on *motzai* Shabbos?

The *b'racha* is still omitted now (see question 379).

397. If there is bread on the table when reciting *havdalah*, should it be covered?

Yes, one should cover the bread as one does when reciting *kiddush*.

398. If a person wishes to eat bread immediately after *havdalah*, should the after-*b'racha* be said on the wine?

Yes. If he forgot to say the after-*b'racha*, it should not be said during the meal. He should have in mind when *bensching* at the end of the meal that he wants the *bensching* to include the wine.

399. Is one obligated to eat bread in place of the missed *melave malka* meal?

No, there is no obligation to eat bread.

Chapter Nineteen
The Tenth of Av

400. Which restrictions apply after the fast?

In a regular year, the laws of the nine days continue after the fast until *halachic* noon on the tenth of Av. Therefore, one may not bathe, launder, wear fresh clothes, make or buy new clothes, have a haircut, listen to music, eat meat, drink wine, or recite the *b'racha shehecheyanu*.

401. Why do these restrictions continue after the fast?

The first holy Temple was set on fire in the afternoon of the ninth of Av, but continued to burn throughout the tenth of Av. Although the fast was fixed on the ninth when the destruction began, the restrictions continue on the tenth when the destruction was complete.

402. Are there any situations where one may be lenient?

- At a *seudas* mitzvah everyone may partake of meat and wine (compare question 146).
- If necessary, one may cut his nails.
- If necessary, one may launder children's clothes.
- It is permitted to take a cold shower, if necessary.

- If one has no more prepared clothes, he may wear freshly laundered clothes.

- A person who is traveling on the tenth of Av should consult a rav regarding laundering clothes for the trip.

403. Are there any differences when Tisha b'Av falls on Thursday?

- It is permitted to launder clothes after the fast if they are needed for Shabbos. Regarding other clothes, some opinions permit one to launder them immediately but some opinions permit this only on Friday morning.

- Haircuts are permitted on Friday morning.

404. When is it permitted to bathe in honor of Shabbos?

On Friday morning.

405. Are there any differences when the fast is postponed to Sunday the tenth of Av?

- Meat and wine are forbidden on Sunday evening, but permitted on Monday morning.

- Some opinions permit listening to music on Sunday evening, but some permit only on Monday morning.

- All other restrictions are lifted immediately after the fast.

Glossary

Aleinu - Prayer recited at the conclusion of *shacharis, mincha* and *ma'ariv.*

Aneinu - Prayer added to *shemoneh esrei* on a fast day.

Ashrei - Psalm 145, recited during *shacharis.*

Ashkenaz - German or Polish Jewry.

Avinu malkeinu - Prayer recited on fast days after *shemoneh esrei.*

Bensch - To recite grace after meals.

Bimah - Table upon which the Torah is placed when reading.

Borei p'ri hagafen - *B'racha* recited over wine and grape juice (lit. who creates the fruit of the vine).

B'racha (pl. *brachos*) - A blessing.

Bris - Circumcision.

Chazan - The man who leads the prayer service.

Chosson and kallah - Newly married couple.

Chutz La'aretz - The Diaspora.

Cohen (pl. *Cohanim*) - Priest.

Daven - To pray.

Devarim - The book of Deuteronomy.

Eicha - Lamentations.

Eiruv - Enclosure of a public domain which transfers it into a private one in order to permit objects to be carried on Shabbos.

Eretz Yisroel - The land of Israel.

Erev Rosh Chodesh - The day before the first day of the Jewish lunar month.

Erev Shabbos - The day before Shabbos.

Erev Tisha b'Av - The day before Tisha b'Av.

Fleishig - Meaty.

Gabbai - Person who assists in the running of shul services.

Haftarah - Public reading from Prophets.

Hagomeil - Blessing of thanks recited after escaping danger.

Halacha (pl. *halachos*) - Jewish law.

Halachic dawn - 72 *halachic* minutes before sunrise.

Halachic hour - 1/12 day, reckoned from sunrise to sunset (or dawn to nightfall).

Halachic midday - The midpoint between sunrise and sunset.

Hamavdil - The main *b'racha* of *havdalah*.

Hashem - G-d.

Hatov vehameitiv - Blessing recited when more than one person benefits from a new item (compare *shehecheyanu*).

Havdalah - Prayer recited at the conclusion of Shabbos and Yom Tov to divide between a holy day and a weekday.

Kaddish - Prayer that calls for the exaltation of G-d, recited by the *chazan* and by mourners.

Kaddish tiskabel - The *kaddish* recited at the conclusion of the service.

Kebeitza - A volume measure (approx. 60ml).

Kel malei rachamim - Memorial prayer.

Kezayis (pl. *kezaysim*) - A volume measure (approx. 30ml).

Kiddush - Sanctification of Shabbos and Yom Tov, usually recited over a cup of wine.

Kiddush levana - Sanctification of the new moon.

Kinnah (pl. *Kinnos*) - Elegy.

Korbanos - Section of *shacharis* describing the offering of sacrifices.

Lamnatzeach - Psalm 20, recited towards the conclusion of *shacharis*.

Ma'ariv - The evening prayer.

Mayim acharonim - The water with which the hands are washed immediately prior to *bensching*.

Melaveh malka - Meal eaten after Shabbos.

Midrash - Commentary on the Bible.

Mikveh - Ritual immersion pool.

Minyan - Quorum of men required for communal prayer.

Mincha - The afternoon prayer.

Mincha ketana - Two and a half *halachic* hours before sunset.

Mishkan - The Tabernacle that was built in the wilderness.

Mishnah - The basis of the oral law.

Mitzvah (pl. *Mitzvos*) - A commandment.

Mohel - The man who performs the *bris*.

Moshe Rabbeinu - Moses our teacher.

Moshiach - The messiah.

Motzai Shabbos - The day after Shabbos.

Motzai Tisha b'Av - The day after Tisha b'Av.

Mussar - Ethics.

Niddah - Menstruant.

Pidyon haben - Redemption of the firstborn.

Pirkei Avos - Ethics of the Fathers.

Pitum haketores - Section of *shacharis* describing the frankincense offering.

Posek - *Halachic* authority.

Rabbeinu Tam - Rabbi Yaakov, grandson of *Rashi*, considered to be one of the greatest of the *ba'alei* Tosfos.

Rav (pl. *Rabbonim*) - Rabbi.

Reviyis - Liquid measure (86ml or approx. 3 fl. oz.).

Rosh Chodesh - The first day of the new month.

Sandek - The man who holds the baby at a *bris*.

Sedra - Weekly Torah portion.

Sefer (pl. *Sefarim*) - Book.

Sefer Torah (pl. *Sifrei Torah*) - Hand written scroll of the five books of Moses.

Sephard - Spanish, Portugese, or North African Jewry.

Seuda hamafsekes - The last meal eaten prior to the beginning of the fast.

Seuda shlishis - Third meal that is eaten on Shabbos.

Seudas mitzvah - Meal eaten to celebrate a mitzvah, e.g. wedding, circumcision, redemption of the firstborn etc.

Shacharis - The morning service.

Shaitel - Wig.

Shechina - The Divine presence.

Shehecheyanu - The blessing made to thank Hashem for bringing us to the time when we can benefit from a new item or perform a new mitzvah.

Shemoneh esrei - Supplication that forms a central part of formal prayer. On a weekday this contains 19 blessings.

Sheva brachos - Festive meal held in honor of *chosson* and *kallah*.

Shiva - The week of mourning after the passing of a close relative.

Shulchan Aruch - Code of Jewish law.

Simcha - Joyous occasion.

Siyum - Festive meal made at the conclusion of a tractate etc.

Tachanun - Prayer recited immediately following *shemoneh esrei.*

Tallis - Prayer shawl.

Tallis koton - Small four cornered garment worn by men.

Talmid chochom (pl. *Talmidei chachomim*) - Torah scholar.

Tamei - Spiritually impure.

Tanach - The Bible.

Targum - Authorized Aramaic translation and explanation of the written Torah by the proselyte Onkelos (around 90c.e.).

Tefillin - Phylacteries.

Tehillim - The book of Psalms.

Tzidkascha - Prayer recited during *mincha* on Shabbos.

Tzitzis - Fringes attached to a man's *tallis.*

Uva le'tzyion - Collection of verses recited towards the end of *shacharis.*

Yahrzeit - Hebrew date on which a person passed away.

Yeshiva - Talmudic college.

Zemiros - Shabbos songs.

Zimun - Invitation to *bensch,* made in the presence of at least three men.

Index

Hebrew Sources

ראשי תיבות

הולמבה״מ = הלכות ומנהגי בין המצרים להגרמ״מ קארפ, תשס״א.
יבב״ה = יד בבין המצרים להגרי״ד פלדשטיין, תשנ״ז.
נט״ג = נטע גבריאל להג״ר גבריאל ציננער, ב׳ חלקים, תשנ״ז .
קהבה״מ = קיצור הלכות בין המצרים להגר״ש איידער, תשל״ח.
קע״מ = קרא עלי מועד להה״ר י.ד. ספטימוס, תש״ס.

פרק א - הקדמה

[1] מדרש איכה רבה פ״א ה״ל עה״פ כל רודפיה השיגוה, מ״ב ס׳
תקמט סק״א.   [2] ס׳ תקנא סע׳ א, רמ״א סע׳ ב, ד, ס׳ תקנד, ס׳
תקנד.   [3] צי״א ח״י ס׳ כו בשם החיד״א לגבי שהחיינו ובשם א״א
בוטשאטש לגבי נישואין, שו״ת שבט הלוי ח״ח ס׳ קסח, וע׳ אג״מ
ח״א ס׳ קסח שהתיר נישואין לצורך, ובח״ד ס׳ קיב סע׳ ב התיר
תספורת לצורך גדול.

פרק ב - צום י״ז תמוז

[4] גמ׳ תענית כו: עד כח:.   [5] רמב״ם הל׳ תענית ריש פ״ה, מ״ב
ס׳ תקמט סק״א.   [6] תוספות ריש פ״ג דמגילה, מ״ב סי׳ תקסו ס״ק
יב.   [7] ס׳ תקנ סע׳ א, מ״ב סק״ד, ביה״ל ד״ה הכל חייבים.   [8]
מ״ב סק״ג, ה ושעה״צ סק״ג, תורת היולדת פמ״ז סע׳ א.   [9] שם
סק״ד, ביה״ל ס׳ תקנט סע׳ ט ד״ה ואינו.   [10] ביה״ל ס׳ תקמט,
ועיין שעה״צ ס׳ תקנט ס״ק לד שמסתפק לענין תענית נדחה.   [11]
מ״ב ס׳ תקנ סק״ה.   [12] בשם ר״ח מבריסק.   [13] שם סק״ה.
[14] מט״א ס׳ תרב סע׳ כג.   [15] שו״ת אג״מ או״ח ח״ג ס׳ צא,
צי״א ח״י ס׳ כה פ׳ כב, שש״כ פל״ט סע׳ ח, שבת שבתון סע׳ צח
בהערות שם, תשובות והנהגות ח״ג ס׳ קנו, מבית לוי עמ׳ לה אות
ה.   [16] ס׳ תקסז סע׳ א, מ״ב סק״ו.   [17] מ״ב ס׳ תקסז ס״ק יא,
מט״א ס׳ תרב סע׳ ו, אלף למטה סק״ג.   [18] מנחת יצחק ח״ד ס׳
קט, וע״ש שמתיר להשתמש עם אבק שיניים, בלי מים.   [19] ס׳
תקסד סע׳ א, מ״ב סק״ו, שעה״צ סק״ז.   [20] מ״ב ס׳ פט ס״ק כז,
אשי ישראל פי״ג סע׳ כו והערה עא בשם הגרשז״א.   [21] אלף
המגן ס׳ תרב ס״ק טו.   [22] ס׳ תקסח סע׳ א, מ״ב ס״ק כד, מט״א ס׳
תרב סע׳ כג.   [23] מ״ב שם סק״ג, פסק״ת ס׳ תקסה הע׳ 3.   [24]
ביה״ל ריש ס׳ תקסה.   [25] שם סע׳ ב, מ״ב סק״ו, ז.   [26] רמ״א
סי׳ תקסה סע׳ ג, אשי ישראל פכ״ג הערה רב, מט״א ס׳ תרב סע׳
כה, וצ״ע מה שכתוב בסידורים לומר ׳רבון׳ בתענית יחיד דווקא
דהוי נגד השו״ע ס׳ תקסה סע׳ ד, וע׳ מט״א שם סע׳ ל שאם שכח
לאומרו במנחה שיכול לאומרו במעריב.   [27] דעת תורה ס׳ תקפד
סע׳ א בשם קיצור של״ה.   [28] מ״ב ס׳ תקסה ס״ק יג, אג״מ יו״ד
ח״ג סו״ס כא.   [29] שעה״צ ס׳ תנ סק״ח.

130   Guidelines - The Three Weeks

פרק ג - הג' שבועות (ס' תקנא)

[30] רמ"א סע' ב, מ"ב ס"ק טז, רמ"א סע' ד.   [31] מ"ב שם וס"ק
יט, מבית לוי עמ' ג אות א.   [32] מ"ב שם, שו"ת שבט הלוי ח"ח ס'
קכז (ב), שו"ת משנה הלכות ח"ו סי' קט, א"ר ס"ק כו, ארחות רבינו
ח"ב עמ' קכח אות ט, ולגבי מי שסובל מדכאון, י"א שמותר לשמוע
שירים, וצריך שאלת חכם.   [33] יבב"ה פ"ז סע' טז, שו"ת ציץ
אליעזר חט"ז ס' יט.   [34] כה"ח אות מא, שו"ת שבה"ל שם,
הגר"ח קניבסקי הובא ביבב"ה פ"ז ס"ק טז.   [35] קהבה"מ פ"ב A 3,
קע"מ פ"ב הערה יא, הומבה"מ פ"ג הע' 13, נט"ג פט"ו סע' יג,
נחמת ישראל פ"ב סעיף יא.   [36] מ"ב ס"ק טז, קע"מ פ"ב הע' יב.
[37] מ"ב ס"ק עט, מבית לוי עמ' ה אות א.   [38] מ"ב ס"ק פב.
[39] מבית לוי עמ' ו אות ב, חנוך לנער פכ"א הע' א, יבב"ה פ"ח
סע' ט בשם הגר"ח קניבסקי.   [40] אג"מ או"ח ח"ד ס' קב, חו"מ
ח"א סוף ס' צג, מעדני שלמה עמ' נא.   [41] מ"ב סק"פ, קש"ע ס'
קכב סע' ד, וע' הומבה"מ פ"ג הע' 21 שדחה שיטה זו.   [42] סע'
יב, קהבה"מ פ"ב 5 B בשם הגרמ"פ.   [43] יבב"ה פ"ח סע' ה בשם
הגר"ש ואזנר.   [44] מ"ב סק"ד, שעה"צ סק"ד, קש"ע ס' קכב סע'
טו, נודב"י קמא או"ח ס' כח, כה"ח אות י, וע"ע מבית לוי עמ' ו
אות ו שאוסר בעל ברית להסתפר, שו"ת בנין ציון ס' לא.   [45]
שו"ת חת"ס או"ח ס' קנח.   [46] יבב"ה פ"ח סע' יד בשם הגר"נ
קרליץ, שעהמ"ב ס' קכ סע' ח בקונט'א.   [47] מ"ב ס"ק פז, שעה"צ
ס"ק צג.   [48] מ"ב סק"כ.   [49] שם.   [50] מ"ב ס"ק צח, שעה"צ
ס"ק צט, וע' מבית לוי עמ' ז אות א שכ' שמנהג א"י להחמיר לא
לברך כלל אף בשבת כדעת האריז"ל הובא במג"א.   [51] רמ"א
סע' יז, מ"ב ס"ק קא, מבית לוי עמ' ז אות ב.   [52] מ"ב ס"ק צט,
ובס' קע"מ בהערות הגרח"ק סק"ק כ' שכיון שאוכל מפני פקוח
נפש, שחושש שמא ימות אם לא יאכל, לא שייך לומר שהחיינו
לזמן הזה.   [53] מ"ב ושעה"צ שם, וע' קש"ע ס' קכב סע' ב.   [54]
אג"מ או"ח ח"ג ס' פ ד"ה ומכונית חדשה, וכ"כ בהומבה"מ פ"ג
הערה 26, דלא הותרה ברכת שהחיינו אלא בדבר שאין בו שמחה
יתירה ולכן לא מברכים על בגד חדש, אבל מברכים על פרי חדש.
[55] סע' יז, דעת תורה.   [56] מ"ב ס' רכג סק"ב, יבב"ה פ"ט סע'
יא, וע' הליכות שלמה פכ"ג סע' י שאין לברך ברכה זו כלל.   [57]
מ"ב ס"ק מה, מבית לוי עמ' ח אות ד, קש"ע ס' קכב סע' ב.   [58]
אג"מ או"ח ח"ג ס' פ, שעמב"ה ס' קכב ס"ק יא.   [59] אג"מ שם
ד"ה ומכונית, מבית לוי הנ"ל.   [60] מ"ב ס"ק יב, פסקי תשובות
אות 84.   [61] מעדני שלמה עמ' נז, טעמא דקרא אות מא בשם
בחזו"א.   [62] א"ר סק"ד, מבית לוי עמ' ח אות ד, וע' אג"מ או"ח
ח"ד סו"ס פב.   [63] סע' יח.   [64] שם, מבית לוי עמ' י אות ח.
[65] מבית לוי עמ' ח אות ו, ארחות רבינו ח"ב עמ' קכט אות יב,

וע' תשובות והנהגות ח"ב ס' רסג.

פרק ד - תשעת הימים (ס' תקנא)

[66] מג"א ס' תקנא ס"ק כו, פרמ"ג שם.   [67] סע' ב, ג, ז, ט, טז,
כה"ח סק"א, וע' שמות רבה ט"ו, כ"א.   [68] מ"ב ס"ק יב, מבית לוי
עמוד ט אות ד, הומבה"מ פ"ד סע' ד.   [69] שם.   [70] אבילות
החורבן עמ' 144.   [71] מ"ב ס"ק יב, קהבה"מ פ"ג B 3, כה"ח ס"ק
כה, מבית לוי עמ' י אות ד, אבילות החורבן עמ' 143, וע' עמ' 144.
[72] מבית לוי עמ' ט אות ד.   [73] קע"מ פ"ד סע' ו, מבית לוי עמ'
יא אות ט, יבב"ה פי"ב סע' טו בשם שלמת חיים ס' שלב.   [74] סע'
ב, רבב"א ח"א סי' שעד, מבית לוי עמ' י אות ה, הומבה"מ פ"ד הע'
12, יבב"ה פי"ב סע' יח.

פרק ה - כיבוס בט' הימים (ס' תקנא)

[75] סע' ג.   [76] מבית לוי עמוד יג אות א.   [77] רמ"א סע' ג.
[78] מ"ב ס"ק מ"ג, שעה"צ ס"ק מד.   [79] מ"ב ס"ק פב, קע"מ פ"ד
הע' ד בשם הגרנ"ק.   [80] יבב"ה פי"ג סע' כד בשם הגרמ"פ.   [81]
רמ"א סע' ג, מ"ב ס"ק לב, כט, מבית לוי עמ' יד אות ב*, שמעתי
מאת הגרח"ו, וע' פ"ת יו"ד ס' שפא סק"ג וגשר החיים ח"א עמ'
רלד, אמנם ע' הומבה"מ פ"ד הע' 18 שכ' שנוהגין להחמיר.   [82]
מ"ב ס"ק פג.   [83] קע"מ שם.   [84] מבית לוי עמ' יג אות א, קע"מ
פ"ד הע' א בשם הגרנ"ק, יבב"ה פי"ג סע' יא.   [85] שם.   [86] כן
נראה פשוט, דהוי כבגדים דמלפפים בהם תמיד.   [87] פסקי
תשובות אות כ, מבית לוי עמ' יג אות א.   [88] קע"מ שם, יבב"ה
פי"ג סע' יב.   [89] שלמת חיים ס' שלב אסר, ארחות רבינו ח"ב
עמ' קלב קלב אות יא נשאר בצ"ע, אג"מ ח"ג סו"ס פ מתיר להשחיר
אבל להבריק התיר רק לכב' שבת, מבית לוי עמ' טז אות י, וע'
הומבה"מ פ"ד סע' כג.   [90] סע' ג.   [91] סע' ג, יו"ד ס' שפט סע'
א, וש"ך סק"ב.   [92] ש"ך שם סק"ד, כה"ח סק"צ.   [93] קע"מ פ"ד
הע' ז בשם הגריש"א.   [94] שמעתי מהגר"ח ובר.   [95] מ"ב סק"ו
בשם הגר"א, וכן המנהג.   [96] מ"ב ס"ק מה, אג"מ או"ח ח"ג סי' פ.
[97] מנח"י ח"י סו"ס מד, כה"ח ס"ק צא, ארחות רבינו ח"ב עמ' קל
אות יח החמירו, מבית לוי עמ' יד אות ב, קהבה"מ פ"ג D 7 בשם
הגרמ"פ, שלמת חיים ס' שלא הקילו. מ"ב ס"ק מה.   [98] עיין ספר
נחמת ישראל פי"ז הערה 198 שמחמיר מגיל שש, אבל שמענו
מהגר"י טשזנר שאין להחמיר כ"כ, וע'י מ"ב ס"ק פב שדוקא בשבוע
שחל בו ולא מר"ח.   [99] מנח"י שם, וע' פסקי תשובות הע' 103,
אבילות החורבן עמ' 152 בהערה, שו"ת אבני ישפה ח"ג ס' נח.
[100] קע"מ פ"ד סע' ט, קהבה"מ פ"ג D 10, יבב"ה פי"ד סע' ז בשם
הגריש"א, הומבה"מ פ"ד סע' כט.   [101] רמ"א סע' א, הומבה"מ
פ"ד סע' לב.   [102] קע"מ פ"ד הע' יח, מבית לוי עמ' מ אות ה.

[103] שם, יבב"ה פכ"א סע' כ.   [104] מ"ב סק"ג, ד, שע"ת סק"א,
הומבה"מ פ"ד סע' לב, מבית לוי עמ' כא אות יב, וע' נט"ג פל"ג סע'
ח.   [105] אבילות החורבן עמ' 153, נט"ג פל"ג סע' י.   [106] יבב"ה
פי"ד סע' כא, פכ"א סע' יב, נט"ג פל"ג סע' יב.   [107] קע"מ פ"ד
הע' יג בשם החזו"א, יבב"ה פי"ד סע' יז בשם הגרשז"א, הומבה"מ
פ"ד הע' 44* בשם הגריש"א, שו"ת שבט הלוי ח"ט ס' קלא (ד),
ובנט"ג פל"ג סע' יג כתב שלא.   [108] א"א מבוטשאטש ריש
הסימן.   [109] מ"ב סק"ק לג, רמ"א סע' ג.   [110] מבית לוי עמ' טז
אות ט, מנחת יצחק ח"י ס' מד.   [111] סע' ג, ט"ז סק"ד, קהבה"מ
פ"ג D 9.   [112] שם.

פרק ו - עשיית וקניית בגדים בט' הימים

[113] סע' ז, ח, מ"ב ס"ק מח, קהבה"מ בשם הגרמ"פ פ"ג E 4,
מבית לוי עמ' יא סע' ב.   [114] רמ"א סע' ז, מ"ב ס"ק נב, ביה"ל
ד"ה ונהגו.   [115] מ"ב ס"ק מו וס"ק יד.   [116] פסקי תשובות הע'
160, בצל החכמה ח"ד ס' נד, יבב"ה פט"ז סע' יא.   [117] קהבה"מ
פ"ג E 5, יבב"ה פט"ז סע' ה, ו, מבית לוי עמ' יג אות ז, שו"ת שבט
הלוי ח"י ס' פה (ה), וע' קע"מ פ"ד סע' יב בשם החזו"א.   [118]
רמ"א סע' ז.   [119] נט"ג פל"ז סע' ב, פסקי תשובות הע' 157.
[120] יבב"ה פט"ז סע' יב בשם הגרנ"ק.   [121] רמ"א סע' ז, מ"ב
ס"ק מה, מט.   [122] שע"ת סק"י.   [123] ערוה"ש ס"ק יט.   [124]
אג"מ ח"ג ס' פ, שעמב"ה ס' קכב ס"ק יא.   [125] נט"ג פל"א סע' ט.
[126] פמ"ג א"א סוסק"ז, וע' מ"ב ס' תקנד ס"ק מח ודו"ק.   [127]
אג"מ שם.   [128] רבב"א ח"א ס' שעב בשם הגר"ש ואזנר, יבב"ה
פט"ו סע' ה, נט"ג פל"א סע' ב.   [129] מבית לוי עמ' י אות ז, אג"מ
אה"ע ח"ד ס' פד סק"א, יבב"ה פט"ו סע' יג, נט"ג פל"א סע' יג.
[130] אג"מ ח"ג ס' פ ד"ה ומכונית, מבית לוי עמ' ח אות ד.   [131]
יבב"ה פט"ו סע' ו בשם הגרנ"ק, לקט יושר עמ' קז ענין א.   [132]
קע"מ פ"ד סע' יג בשם הגרנ"ק.

פרק ז - בשר ויין בט' הימים (ס' תקנא)

[133] סע' ט, כל בו ס' סב, ערוה"ש ס"ק כג, מ"ב ס"ק סה.   [134]
סע' י.   [135] מ"ב ס"ק סג.   [136] מ"ב שם, נט"ג פל"ח סע' ה.
[137] מ"ב סק"ע ושעה"צ ס"ק עו, קע"מ פ"ה הע' י בשם הגר"ש
ואזנר, חנוך לנער פכ"א הע' ה, הומבה"מ פ"ד הע' 60 בשם
הגריש"א, ערוה"ש ס"ק כו.   [138] מ"ב ס"ק סד.   [139]
ערוה"ש ס"ק כו, הומבה"מ פ"ד סע' מו, מ"ב ס"ק סא, סד.   [140]
רמ"א סע' ט, מ"ב ס"ק נו, קהבה"מ פ"ג C 3.   [141] אג"מ או"ח
ח"ד ס' כא סוף סק"ד.   [142] מ"ב ס' רן סוסק"ב, ששכ"כ פמ"ב סע'
סא, נחמת ישראל פכ"ב הערה 293 בשם הרבה פוסקים, שו"ע ס'
רי סע' ב.   [143] אג"מ הנ"ל.   [144] מ"ב ס"ק נח.   [145] רמ"א

סע' ט, י, מ"ב ס"ק סב, יד אפרים על מג"א ס"ק לג. [146] מ"ב ס"ק
עה, עז, עח, שעה"צ ס"ק פט. [147] סידור פסח כהלכתו פי"ד סע'
ו, אג"מ ח"א ס' קנז, שו"ת משנה הלכות ח"ו ס' קסו. [148] מ"ב
ס"ק עג, וע' שו"ת שבה"ל ח"ו ס' עב, וערוה"ש סע' כח. [149]
שו"ת שבה"ל ח"י ס' פא (ט). [150] נט"ג פל"ח סע' ו. [151] אג"מ
או"ח ח"ד ס' קיב סע' ג. [152] ס' תקנא סע' ט, כל בו ס' סב,
ערוה"ש ס"ק כג. [153] מ"ב ס"ק סו. [154] מ"ב ס"ק נז. [155]
רמ"א סע' יא, הומבה"מ פ"ד סע' מח והע' 73 בסוף, יבב"ה פי"ח
סע' ח. [156] באה"ט סוס"ק כט, קע"מ פ"ה הע' ז בשם הגרנ"ק,
הומבה"מ עמ' עט הע' 74 בסוף בשם הגריש"א, יבב"ה שם סע' ט,
י. [157] מ"ב ס"ק נט, שו"ע ס' תקנב סע' י. [158] סע' י ורמ"א,
מ"ב סק"ע, קע"מ פ"ה הע' ג, ה, הומבה"מ פ"ד הע' 74* ד"ה ובגדר,
פסקי תשובות הע' 179, 180. [159] קע"מ שם הע' ג, ע"פ מ"ב ס'
רעא ס"ק סז ושו"ע ס' קצ סע' ג. [160] הומבה"מ פ"ד הע' 74* ד"ה
ולכו"ע, נט"ג פל"ט סע' יא. [161] נט"ג שם סע' ט ע"פ מ"ב ס'
ער"ב ס"ק כז. [162] מ"ב ס"ק נח. [163] מ"ב ס"ק עב. [164]
אוצר הברית ח"א עמ' רצד סע' ד, נט"ג פ"מ סע' יא. [165] שו"ת
שבט הלוי ח"ו ס' קלא (א).

פרק ח - רחיצה בט' הימים (ס' תקנא)

[166] סע' טז ורמ"א ומ"ב ס"ק צד. [167] ס' תקנד סע' ט, ערוה"ש
ס' תקנא ס"ק לז. [168] אג"מ אה"ע ח"ד ס' פד סק"ד, יבב"ה פ"כ
סע' יד בשם הגריש"א, מבית לוי עמ' טז אות א, קע"מ פ"ג הע' ה,
ו, וע' מ"ב ס' תריג סק"א. [169] קע"מ פ"ג בהערות הגרח"ק ס"ק
טז בשם הגריש"א, יבב"ה פ"כ סע' י. [170] מ"ב ס"ק פח, צג.
[171] רמ"א סע' טז, מ"ב ס"ק פט, צו, ביה"ל ד"ה בחפיפת,
קהבה"מ פ"ג 7 F, נט"ג פמ"ג סע' ב. [172] מ"ב ס"ק פח, שעה"צ
ס"ק צד. [173] רמ"א סע' טז, מ"ב ס"ק צב, מבית לוי עמ' טז הע' ו,
וע' ביה"ל ד"ה אם. [174] מ"ב ס"ק צה, שעה"צ ס"ק צח, מבית
לוי עמ' טז אות ב, כה"ח ס"ק קצ, פסקי תשובות הע' 254 בשם
תוס' חיים על חיי"א כלל קלג ס"ק לז. [175] ערוה"ש ס"ק לה,
מ"ב ס"ק פח, קהבה"מ פ"ג 4 F, מעדני שלמה עמ' נו. [176] סע'
א, ערוה"ש סק"ט וסוף ס"ק יא, מג"א סק"ב והגהות חת"ס שם.
[177] רמ"א סע' ח, וס' תכו סע' ב, ומ"ב שם סק"ח, מעשה רב אות
קנט, ערוה"ש ס"ק כב, הליכות שלמה ח"א פט"ו הע' 22.

פרק ט - ערב ט' באב (ס' תקנב)

[178] סע' יב. [179] רמ"א סו"ס תקנג, מ"ב סק"ח, ט, וביה"ל שם,
הומבה"מ פ"ו סע' א, קע"מ פ"ו הע' ד. [180] ס' תקנב סע' ט
ורמ"א, מ"ב ס"ק כב. [181] סע' ז, מ"ב ס"ק יז, גר"א ד"ה וא"צ.
[182] מ"ב ס"ק יז, שע"ת, הג' רעק"א בשם מהריק"ש, תורת

היולדת פמ"ח סע' יב.   [183] רמ"א שם, מ"ב ס"ק יח.   [184] סע'
ה, ו, ורמ"א, מ"ב ס"ק יג, טז, באה"ט סק"ז.   [185] סע' ו, באה"ט
סק"ה, קע"מ פ"ו הע' ט בשם הגרנ"ק, הומבה"מ פ"ו סע' יא.   [186]
סע' א, ד, מ"ב ס"ק יג, רמ"א סע' א, הומבה"מ שם סע' ט.   [187]
סע' ו, מ"ב סק"ד, שעה"צ סק"א, יבב"ה פכ"ד סע' יז, הומבה"מ פ"ו
סע' י.   [188] סע' ח, מ"ב ס"ק יט.   [189] ס' תקנג סע' א, מ"ב
סק"ב.   [190] מ"ב ס"ק יח.

פרק י - איסור אכילה ושתייה בט' באב

[191] ס' תקנ סע' א, ס' תקנד סע' א, כ, כב, ס' תקנט סע' ג, ע'
גרי"ז על הרמב"ם הל' תעניות ד"ה והנראה.   [192] רמב"ם הל'
תענית פ"ה ה"ג הובא במ"ב ס' תקמט סק"ב, גמ' תענית כט..
[193] ס' תקנ סע' א, ערוה"ש סי' תקנד סע' ז.   [194] מ"ב ס' תקנ
סק"ה, קע"מ פ"ט הע' א.   [195] ס' תקנ סע' א ברמ"א, מבית לוי
עמ' לה אות ז, תורת היולדת פמ"ח סע' ד, ו.   [196] ס' תקנד סע'
ו, רמ"א מ"ב סק"ט, ביה"ל ס' תקנט סע' ט ד"ה ואינו.   [197] תורת
היולדת פמ"ח סע' ב, ג ע"פ ערוה"ש ס' ח, מבית לוי עמ' לה אות
ט, י ע"פ הרמ"א.   [198] קע"מ פ"ט הע' ו בשם הגרנ"ק, מבית לוי
עמ' לד הע' א.   [199] מבית לוי עמ' לו אות יג.   [200] ס' תקנד
סע' ה, תורת היולדת פמ"ח סע' ד.   [201] תורת היולדת פמ"ח סע'
ד והע' ז, יבב"ה פכ"ה סע' ד בשם החזו"א, מבית לוי עמ' לו אות
יא, יבב"ה שם סע' ג בשם הגרנ"ק.   [202] שיעורין של תורה
שיעורי המצוות אות כא, כב, כג, כט, וכן שמעתי מהגרצ"ו.   [203]
שש"כ פל"ט סע' כו.   [204] ס' תריח סע' ח, מ"ב ס"ק כא, ביה"ל
ד"ה ואם אמדוהו.   [205] מ"ב ס' תקנ סק"ד, ס' תקנד ס"ק יא,
ביה"ל ס' תקנט סע' ט ד"ה ואינו.   [206] אלף המגן ס' תריח סק"א.
[207] ס' תקנד סע' ו, מבית לוי עמ' לד הע' א, יבב"ה פכ"ה סע' יז.
[208] ס' תקנד סע' ה.   [209] שו"ת אג"מ או"ח ח"ג ס' צא, שש"כ
פל"ט סע' ח, שבת שבתון סע' צח בהערות שם.   [210] ס' תקסז
סע' א, מ"ב סק"ד.   [211] מ"ב שם ס"ק יא.   [212] מנחת יצחק
ח"ד ס' קט, וע"ש שמתיר להשתמש עם אבק שיניים, בלי מים.
[213] אלף המגן ס' תרב סק"ט טו.   [214] ס' תקסח סע' א, מ"ב ס"ק
כד.   [215] עיין מקורות 385.   [216] שש"כ פס"ב הע' קח בשם
הגרש"ז, הומבה"מ פ"ז הע' 71* בשם הגריש"א, ודלא כשו"ת שבט
הלוי ח"ט סי' קלג (ב) שאוסר לאכול לפני הנחתן.

פרק יא - רחיצה וסיכה בט' באב (ס' תקנד)

[217] סע' ז.   [218] סע' ט.   [219] מ"ב ס' תריג סק"ב.   [220] סע'
י.   [221] סע' יא.   [222] רמ"א סע' ט, מט"א ס' תריג סע' ה.
[223] סע' ט, וע' סי' ד מ"ב ס"ק מא שמקומות אלה אינן משום רוח
רעה אלא משום נקיות.   [224] ס' תריג סע' ג, מ"ב סק"ו.   [225]

רמ"א שם, מ"ב סק"ז.   [226] מבית לוי עמ' כו אות ט.   [227] ע'
רמ"א תרטז סע' ב, והנט"ג פס"ט סע' ב סתם להחמיר, מט"א ס'
תרט"ז סע' ב, אלף למטה סק"ב.   [228] מ"ב ס' תקנד ס"ק יט, וכן
שמעתי מהגרגר"ץ, פרמ"ג א"א ס"ק יא.   [229] מ"ב ס' תקנד ס"ק
כט, ודלא כיוה"כ.   [230] מ"ב ס"ק כא.   [231] ס' תקנא שעה"צ
ס"ק לה.   [232] עיין מקורות 173.   [233] ס' תקנד סע' טו, מ"ב
ס"ק כח, כט, ביה"ל ד"ה סיכה, נט"ג פע"ג סע' ה בשם הגרמ"פ.
[234] מ"ב ס"ק כט, יבב"ה פכ"ז סע' יח, נט"ג פע"ג סע' ט, אבל ע'
בהומבה"מ פ"ז הע' 39 שתמה ע"ז.   [235] ס' תקנט סע' ז, מ"ב ס"ק
כז, הומבה"מ פ"ז סע' סג.

פרק יב - נעילת הסנדל בט' באב (ס' תקנד)

[236] סע' טז.   [237] מ"ב ס"ק לא.   [238] הליכות שלמה ח"ב פ"ה
סע' טז.   [239] קע"מ פ"ח סע' ז והע' יא, מבית לוי עמ' כו אות יב.
[240] חלקת יעקב או"ח ס' ריח.   [241] ס' תריד סע' ג, תורת
היולדת פנ"ב הע' לו.   [242] חכ"א כלל קנב סע' יז, יבב"ה פכ"ח
סע' ו בשם הגרנ"ק, קע"מ פ"ח סע' ח והע' יג.   [243] ס' תקנד סע'
יח, מ"ב ס"ק לז, שעה"צ ס"ק מד, פסקי תשובות אות יז בשם שו"ת
אז נדברו ח"ח ס' סא.

פרק יג - לימוד התורה בט' באב (ס' תקנד)

[244] סע' א.   [245] סע' ג, מ"ב סק"ה.   [246] רבב"א ח"ב ס' קנה
סע' יד, נט"ג פע"ה סע' ג.   [247] סע' א, מ"ב סק"ב.   [248]
הומבה"מ פ"ז סע' מב, יבב"ה פכ"ט הע' ה, וע' מ"ב ס' תקנא ס"ק
פא, שעה"צ ס"ק צא.   [249] סע' א, ב, מ"ב סק"ב, ג, נט"ג פע"ה
סע' ה סע' ו, פסקי תשובות אות ב.   [250] מ"ב סק"ח.   [251]
מאירי מו"ק כא/א ד"ה אלו דברים, מבית לוי עמ' כט אות א,
יבב"ה פכ"ז סע' י, רבב"א ח"א ס' שפו בשם הגרח"ק, וע'
הומבה"מ פ"ז הע' 57 בשם הגריש"א דלא כגרח"ק.   [252] מ"ב
סק"ד, ערוה"ש סק"ד, קע"מ פ"ח הערות הגרח"ק ס"ק לב בשם
החזו"א, יבב"ה פכ"ט הע' יג.   [253] קע"מ שם הע' ג.   [254]
שע"ת סו"ס תקנד, קע"מ שם.   [255] הומבה"מ פ"ז הע' 59, קע"מ
שם, פסקי תשובות אות א.   [256] פרמ"ג א"א ס' תקפד ושו"ת
דברי מלכיאל ח"ו סי' ט התירו דרך בקשה ותחינה וכן התיר
הגר"ש ואזנר הובא בקע"מ פ"ח הע' ט, ובשם הגרמ"פ אסר,
ובהערות הגרח"ק בשם החזו"א שאולי התיר רק לנשים, מ"ב ס'
תקנד סק"ז ושעה"צ סק"ח.   [257] הומבה"מ פ"ז סע' מו, יסוד
ושורש העבודה שער ט פי"ב, רבבות אפרים ח"א ס' שפ אות ד,
יבב"ה פכ"ט סע' יד, וע' קע"מ פ"ח הע' ח בשם הגרנ"ק והגרח"ק
שיש לדלג כמה דברים.   [258] מ"ב סק"ה, הומבה"מ פ"ז סע' מג
והע' שם.

פרק יד - שאילת שלום בט' באב (ס' תקנד)

[259] סע' כ, מ"ב ס"ק מא. [260] שם. [261] שם וס"ק מב, אבילות החורבן עמ' 193. [262] פשוט. [263] שו"ת שמלת חיים יו"ד ס' תריח. [264] מבית לוי עמ' כז אות טו, קע"מ פ"ח הע' כד בשם הגרנ"ק. [265] נט"ג פע"ו סע' ז, שו"ת הר צבי יו"ד ס' רצ. [266] הליכות שלמה ח"א פרק ב סוס"ק כו. [267] שם סע' ו. [268] פסקי תשובות אות יט. [269] כה"ח ס"ק צא. [270] שו"ת התעוררות תשובה שם.

פרק טו - מלאכה בט' באב

[271] ס' תקנד סע' כב ורמ"א, מ"ב ס"ק מט, קשו"ע ס' קכד סע' טו. [272] תוס' חיים על חיי"א כלל קלה ס"ק יט הובא בכה"ח ס"ק קו ויבב"ה פל"ב סע' יב, סע' כב, קשו"ע שם, סע' כד, מ"ב ס"ק מט, נ. [273] סע' כב, מ"ב ס"ק מו. [274] מ"ב ס"ק מח, שעה"צ סק"נ. [275] ס' תקנט סע' י, ערוה"ש סוס"ע ט'. [276] מבית לוי עמ' לח אות ב, ברכי יוסף ס' תקנט סק"ז.

פרק טז - ישיבה על כסא בט' באב

[277] ס' תקנט סע' ג, מ"ב סק"י. [278] מ"ב ס"ק יב. [279] מ"ב ס"ק יא, שע"ת תקנב סק"ג (ח'). [280] טעמי המנהגים ס' תתרסד, הומבה"מ פ"ז סע' סה, יבב"ה פ"ל סע' ג, וע' קע"מ פ"ח הע' כב שהחזו"א לא הקפיד על השיעור, ארחות רבינו ח"ב כמ' קלח אות יב, וכ"כ בהומבה"מ הע' 92 ד"ה ושיעור גובה בשם הגריש"א. [281] תורת היולדת פמ"ח סע' יב, יבב"ה פ"ל סע' ז. [282] קע"מ פ"ח ס"ק כב בשם הגרשז"א, תורת היולדת שם הע' יז בשם הגריש"א, הומבה"מ פ"ז סע' סז. [283] שע"ת ס' תקנד סק"ח. [284] ס' תקנה סע' ב ורמ"א, ארחות רבינו ח"ב עמ' קלח אות ח. [285] רמ"א, מ"ב ס"ק ז. [286] ע' פסקי תשובות הע' 11 בשם שבט הקהתי ח"ב ס' קצא. [287] רמ"א שם, ס' תקנד סע' כא, ערוה"ש יו"ד ס' שפד סע' ט.

פרק יז - תפילות בט' באב (ס' תקנט)

[288] רמ"א סע' ב, איכה רבה ב', כב. [289] לוח א"י. [290] כה"ח ס"ק יט. [291] נט"ג פנ"ד סע' ה. [292] סע' ג, מ"ב ס"ק טו. [293] שם. [294] מ"ב ס"ק יד, ב"י הובא בכה"ח ס"ק כה. [295] הומבה"מ פ"ט סע' ג, נט"ג פנ"ד הע' י. [296] מ"ב ס"ק כד. [297] הומבה"מ פ"ט הע' ב, יבב"ה פל"ד סע' ב, נט"ג הע' א בשם הגרמ"פ. [298] עיין מקורות 375. [299] מ"ב סק"יד, רמ"א סע' א. [300] סע' ג, ט"ז סק"ד, נט"ג פס"ח הע' ו, מועדים וזמנים ח"ה סי' שמא, וע' יבב"ה פ"ל סק"ט שאין חיוב לשבת ע"ג קרקע דווקא. [301] אשי ישראל פמ"ד הע' קכב. [302] רמ"א סע' ב, מ"ב ס' תצ ס"ק יט, לוח א"י. [303] הלכה ומנהג עמ' 54 סע' מב בשם הגר"ש דבליצקי.

[304] הומבה"מ פ"ט סע' ד, נט"ג פנ"ה סע' ה. [305] הומבה"מ שם.
[306] רמ"א סע' א, מ"ב סק"ב. [307] רמ"א שם. [308] מ"ב סק"ג,
סע' ב, רמ"א סע' ד. [309] רמ"א שם, וגר"א שם. [310] סע' ב,
מ"ב סק"ז. [311] מ"ב סק"ד, ט. [312] הליכות ביתה פכ"ה סע' יט,
תשובות והנהגות ח"ב ס' רנ. [313] מ"ב ס"ק כב, נט"ג פנ"ה סע' ד.
[314] נט"ג סע' יא, והע' כב. [315] מ"ב סק"ה, תשובות והנהגות
הנ"ל, הומבה"מ סע' ד. [316] ס' תקנה סע' א, מ"ב סק"ב,
הומבה"מ פ"ז סע' מז, מ"ב ס' תקנד ס"ק לא ושעה"צ ס"ק לט, לוח
א"י. [317] ערוה"ש ס' תקנד סע' ו, הומבה"מ פ"ט סע' יט. [318]
קע"מ פ"ח הע' לג, יבב"ד פל"ד סע' כא, נט"ג פנ"ח סע' כב, ס'
תקנה, סע' א. [319] רמ"א ס' תקסה סע' ג, לוח א"י, קשו"ע ס' קכד
סי' ג. [320] ס' תקנט סע' ד, רמ"א שם. [321] גשה"ח פכ"ג סע' ג
ס"ק יא, נט"ג פ"ס סע' יא. [322] נט"ג פ"ס סע' טז, יבב"ד פל"ד סע'
לא. [323] כה"ח ס"ק לח, שדי חמד ח"ו עמ' 342 אות ג. [324]
כה"ח סק"מ, נט"ג פ"ס סע' יג, וע"ע בקע"מ פ"ח הע' כד שא"א שום
מי שברך בשחרית. [325] נט"ג סע' יד, הלכה ומנהג עמ' 69 סע'
קמה, קע"מ פ"ח הע' כד, שלא אומרים בשחרית. [326] גשה"ח
ס"פ לא. [327] נט"ג פ"ס סע' יט. [328] הומבה"מ פ"ט סע' כא,
רמ"א סע' ג. [329] טור ס' תקנט. [330] שם, נט"ג פס"א הע' ו.
[331] הומבה"מ שם. [332] סע' ה. [333] נט"ג פס"ח הע' ו, וכן
משמע בקשו"ע קכד, ג. [334] רמ"א סע' ד, קשו"ע ס' קכד סע' ג,
נט"ג פס"ב סע' א. [335] לוח א"י, מ"ב סק"ב. [336] נט"ג פס"ב
סע' ד בשם שו"ת דברי מלכיאל ח"ו סי' ט, וע' הומבה"מ פ"ט הע'
מז. [337] כה"ח ס"ק יט, מ"ב ס"ק טו. [338] סע' ו, מ"ב ס"ק כד.
[339] חיי"א כלל קלה סע' ה, מ"ב ס' תקנד ס"ק כא. [340] ס'
תקנה סע' א. [341] שם, לוח א"י, קע"מ פ"ח סע' כ. [342] קע"מ
פ"ח הע' ח בשם הגרח"ק. [343] ע' מ"ב ס' תקנה סק"ה שאסר,
אבל עי' שו"ת שבט הלוי ח"י ס' פא (ה) שכ' שנוהגין לאמרם, וכ"כ
בהומב"ה פ"ז הע' 71 בשם הגריש"א. [344] קשו"ע ס' קכד סע' יט,
הומבה"מ פ"ט סע' לד. [345] קשו"ע שם. [346] ס' תקנו סע' א
מ"ב סק"ג, הומבה"מ פ"ט סע' לז. [347] מ"ב ס' תקנז סק"ב,
הומבה"מ פ"ז סע' עב, וע"ע במ"ש המג"א ריש הסימן שיכול
לאומרו לפני ועל כולם אבל המ"ב לא הביאו, אבל בנט"ג פ' פ"ה
סע' יח הביאו, וצ"ע. [348] ס' תקסה סע' ב, מ"ב סק"ו, ז. [349]
נט"ג פ' פה סע' יז. [350] ביה"ל ריש סימן תקסה. [351] מ"ב ס'
תקנה סק"ד. [352] מ"ב סי' ל סק"ח, וביה"ל ד"ה אם, וס"ק טו.
[353] לוח א"י, באה"ט ס' תכו סק"ד, ס' תקנו, ס' תקנח ברמ"א.
[354] מ"ב ס' תכו ס"ק יא ושעה"צ סק"ט, מבית לוי עמ' מו הע' א.

פרק יח - ט' באב בשבת או ביום א'

[355] ס' תקנ סע' ג, מ"ב ס' תקנא ס"ק פט, ס' תקנד סק"מ, ס"ק לט,

ס' תקנב סע' י, ס' תקנג סע' ב ברמ״א, ס' תקנו. [356] ס' תקנא סע'
ד, מג״א ס' תקנה סק״ד. [357] מ״ב ס' תקנד סק״מ. [358] פסקי
תשובות ס' תקנד אות יח, אבל ע' הלכה ומנהג עמ' 86 סע' יג
שהתיר אפי' למי שאינו רגיל. [359] רמ״א סו״ס תקנב, וסו״ס תקנג.
[360] פסקי תשובות ס' תקנא אות ה הע' 32, וע' נט״ג פמ״ח הע' ו.
[361] שם, וכן נראה. [362] ס' תקנב סע' י. [363] מ״ב ס״ק כג.
[364] אג״מ ח״ד סי' קיב (א). [365] שע״ת סו״ס תקנג, קע״מ פ״ו
סע' ג. [366] הלכה ומנהג עמ' 87 סע' כ. [367] מ״ב ס' תקנג
סק״ט, י', וביה״ל שם, קשו״ע ס' קכה סע' ד. [368] מבית לוי עמ'
מב אות טו, הלכה ומנהג עמ' 88 סע' ל. [369] מבית לוי עמ' מב
סע' יד. [370] מ״ב ס' תקנב ס״ק כג, כד, ששׁ״כ פכ״ח סע' עז.
[371] פסקי תשובות הע' 35, קע״מ פ״ו סע' יד. [372] מ״ב ס״ק כג.
[373] שעה״צ ס' תקנג סק״ז. [374] רמ״א ס' תקנג סע' ב, הומבה״מ
פ״ח סע' ה. [375] רמ״א שם, מ״ב סק״ו, ז, קע״מ פ״ז סע' א, קע״מ
פ״ו ס״ק כו בשם הגרח״ק, מבית לוי עמ' מב אות א. [376] ששׁ״כ
פס״ב סע' מא. [377] ע' פסקי תשובות ס' תקנג אות ב והערות שם,
יבב״ה פכ״ג סע' ה, הלכה ומנהג עמ' 90 סע' לח. [378] ס' תקנו,
מ״ב סק״א. [379] מ״ב סק״א, ששׁ״כ פס״ב הע' צח, פסקי תשובות
הע' 3. [380] ששׁ״כ שם, קע״מ פ״ז הע' ח, הומבה״מ פ״ח סע' ט
והע' שם. [381] מ״ב סק״א. [382] ס' תקנט סע' ב ורמ״א. [383]
מבית לוי עמ' מג אות ו. [384] שם. [385] ששׁ״כ פס״ב סע' מו,
שבט הלוי ח״ח סו״ס קכט. [386] כה״ח ס' תקנו סק״ט, מנח״י ח״ח
ס' ל, סק״ד. [387] ששׁ״כ פס״ב סע' מו*. [388] קע״מ פ״ז סע' ח
והע' טז, הומבה״מ פ״ח סע' יד והע' 22, מעדני שלמה עמ' נה-נו,
יבב״ה פכ״ג סע' טז. [389] ששׁ״כ פס״ב סע' מו. [390] פסקי
תשובות ס' תקנו הע' 26. [391] שע״ת ס' תקנו סע' א, קע״מ פ״ז
סע' ח, הומבה״מ פ״ח סע' טו, יבב״ה פכ״ג סע' יט. [392] הומבה״מ
פ״ח סע' יג בשם הגריש״א, ארחות רבינו ח״ב עמ' קמה אות מ,
ששׁ״כ פס״ב ס״ק מה, קע״מ פ״ז סע' ז, מבית לוי עמ' מד אות ט.
[393] שו״ת שבט הלוי ח״ח סי' קכט (ג). [394] מ״ב ס' תקנו סק״ג.
[395] ס' תקנו, מבית לוי עמ' מו אות ב. [396] מ״ב סק״ד. [397]
ס' רצט סע' ט. [398] מ״ב שם ס״ק כט. [399] הלכה ומנהג עמ' 96
סע' פ.

פרק יט - י' באב (ס' תקנח)

[400] ס' תקנח ורמ״א, מ״ב סק״ג, נט״ג פ' פח סע' א, קשו״ע ס' קכד
סע' כ. [401] שם ומ״ב סק״א. [402] מ״ב סק״ב, הומבה״מ פ״י
סע' ח, יבב״ה פל״ו סע' יג. [403] מ״ב סק״ג, מבית לוי עמ' לז אות
א, הומבה״מ פ״י סע' יב, פסקי תשובות הערות 18, 20, קע״מ פ״ח
הע' מ. [404] מ״ב סק״ג, מבית לוי שם הע' א. [405] מ״ב סק״ד,
מבית לוי עמ' מו אות ד, פסקי תשובות הע' 13, קהבה״מ פ״ז B 4.

לע"נ

ר' חזקיהו יחיאל
ב"ר אפרים דוד ז"ל

נלב"ע א' מרחשון תשס"ג

ת.נ.צ.ב.ה.

לע"נ

מרת יהודית בת
ר' אהרן ע"ה

נפטרה י' שבט תשס"ג

ת.נ.צ.ב.ה.

May the learning of this ספר be a זכות
for my beloved mother

מרת מלכה בת ישראל ע"ה
(Queenie Ross)

נפטרה ג' דחול המועד פסח תשס"ג

Dedicated by Laurence Ross and family

ת.נ.צ.ב.ה.

לזכרון עולם ולעלוי נשמות

אבי מורי ר' ישראל יצחק בן ר' אברהם יהושע הי"ד
אמי מורתי חנה נעכה בת ר' יוסף הי"ד
אחותי רבקה בת ר' ישראל יצחק הי"ד
אחותי לאה בת ר' ישראל יצחק הי"ד
אחותי הינדא בת ר' ישראל יצחק הי"ד
אחותי הינדל בת ר' ישראל יצחק הי"ד

שנהרגו על קידוש השם ע"י הנאצים ימ"ש

ת.נ.צ.ב.ה.

May the learning of this ספר be a זכות
for our beloved parents

מרת חיה בת ר' פסח ע"ה
מרת מרים בת ר' שרגא ע"ה
ר' שמואל שניאור ב"ר יצחק יעקב ז"ל

Dedicated by the Sherwood family

.ת.נ.צ.ב.ה.

לעילוי נשמת

האי גברא יקירא, מוקיר רבנן,
קובע עיתים לתורה, גומל צדקה וחסד,

הר"ר זישא אלכסנדר
בן ר' פינחס זצ"ל
פלוס

נלב"ע כ"ג בשבט תשנ"ח

.ת.נ.צ.ב.ה.

לע״נ

ר׳ אורי אפרים ז״ל
ב״ר יוסף יצחק פרלמן שליט״א

נפטר בדמי ימיו י״ב טבת תשנ״ו

ת.נ.צ.ב.ה.

לע״נ

מרת מלכה בת ר׳ נתן הלוי ע״ה

נפטרה י׳ תמוז תשס״ב

הונצח ע״י משפחות גודווין וספייער

ת.נ.צ.ב.ה.